IMAGES OF PEACE

Pat Corrick Hinton

WINSTON PRESS

Cover and text design: Evans-Smith and Skubic, Inc.

Photographs by: Camerique—p. 26; NASA—cover (image of world); Vernon
Sigl—p. 60,74; Ned Skubic—cover, pp. 1, 4, 14, 20, 29, 36, 57, 64.

The author and publisher acknowledge the use of excerpts from the
following copyrighted material:
From *Anatomy of an Illness* (excerpts from Chapters 1 and 3), by Norman
Cousins, Copyright © 1979 by W. W. Norton & Company, Inc. Used by
permission of the publisher.
From "Peace Pentecost" by Jim Wallis (*Sojourners,* March 1982) and "On
Loving the Russians" by Joseph Allegretti (*Sojourners,* November 1982).
Reprinted by permission from *Sojourners,* P.O. Box 29272, Washington,
D.C. 20017.

Library of Congress Catalog Card Number: 83-60407

ISBN: 0-86683-748-5

Printed in the United States of America

5   4   3   2   1

Winston Press, Inc.
430 Oak Grove
Minneapolis, Minnesota 55403

To my brother, Bill,

in peace,

and

to all the peacemakers

who shared their creative efforts

in making this book,

especially the Saturday Club

Contents

Preface

Would that even today you knew

the things that make for peace.

—*Luke 19:42, RSV*

Despite worldwide poverty and hunger and threats of nuclear war, many people among us are full of hope. They are inspired and strengthened by their belief that God faithfully takes care of us. But they realize that God expects more from us than trust. God calls us to action. These persons, often quietly, are creatively trying to be peacemakers in everything they do. They are true bearers of the Good News. These peacemakers are not waiting for The Big Powers to achieve The Peace. They know that peace begins in each of us, in our hearts and homes, and that peace, like love, is often hardest to achieve with those closest to us.

The forty reflections in this book feature real peacemakers of today. The stories and comments by and about these peacemakers make it clear that working for peace is not something optional for Christians; it is an indispensable and unmistakable sign of those who take Jesus at his word and truly follow him. These peacemakers have responded to the God who in Scripture calls each of us to work for peace by doing acts of loving service and of justice. But reflection and prayer are necessary for fruitful action. Accordingly, many scriptural passages calling us to peace are included in these pages, and each of the forty reflections closes with a prayer.

From the youngest grade-school child to the nursing-home resident, everyone longs for peace. The creators of peace whose deeds and words are recorded here show that each of us can make a difference. I may not be able to change the whole world, but I can begin to change *my* world.

How wonderful it is to see a messenger coming across the mountains, bringing good news, the news of peace!

—Isaiah 52:7, TEV

*   *   *

Editor's note: The author or origin of each quoted source is given at the end of the quotation. Further information about published works is given, where feasible, in the section entitled Published Sources Used (see pp. 86-88). Items labeled PCH are contributed by the author of this book, as are all the prayers.

IMAGES
OF
PEACE

If we are followers of Jesus, we must be people of peace. But peace awareness doesn't develop all at once. We start to think seriously about peace the moment we take time to listen: when we listen to history, to those of a different generation (old to young and young to old), as well as to those of our own generation; when we listen to our own deeper selves, to God and his message given to us through Jesus; when we listen to those who cry out because they are poor and hungry and treated unjustly.

Part One
Listen and Think About Peace

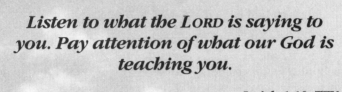

Listen to what the Lord is saying to you. Pay attention of what our God is teaching you.

—Isaiah 1:10, TEV

1. Planting Seeds of Peace

The glory of God is the human person fully alive.

—Irenaeus

Dear Mom:

A marvelous thing is happening to me, and it's due mostly to you and the kind of person you are. I've had to do a lot of soul searching to put this book together. The most important question I've had to ask myself is, Why do I care so much about peace and the things that make for peace that I want to write a book about it? It's marvelous to realize that I care about peace because *you* taught me to care.

Out of many memories, I especially remember the orphans we invited to holiday dinners and how we tried to continue the friendships begun at those meals. I remember the woman you hired to help around the house and the flak you took for it. Little did others know that we hired her, not because we could afford her, but because she needed work. And do you remember the postcards you provided for my home room in high school so we could protest an objectionable movie at a neighborhood theater?

Most of all, I remember all the years you took care of my handicapped brother. Now I realize what it must have cost you to be constantly taking care of his needs for the thirty-nine years he lived. Thirty-nine of your eighty-seven.

Now that you're in your golden years, I'm especially aware of your concern for others. You're so careful never to let anyone be overburdened when they offer to help you, although it often means you go without something you need. And even though your own pain is great most of the time, you don't want the rest of us to strain ourselves helping you. Always looking out for the other person: That seems to be your motto.

And now for the part that means the most to me. It's your serenity. The way you have chosen to live—even in all the difficult times—tells me you're living proof of the words of Jesus: that he has already given you (and all of us) his gift of peace. That's the message you've handed on to me: one of joy and peace because you're so aware of God's presence within you. You're truly one of God's prize creations—giving all that praise to him because you're an authentic human being, full of joy, full of peace, fully alive.

I'm proud of you, Mom. Thank you for sharing your heritage of peace and joy with me, with our whole family, and with everyone who knows you. And thank you for planting the seed of peace for this book years ago.

Lovingly,
your daughter, Pat—PCH

They that are planted in the house of the LORD
    shall flourish in the courts of our God.
They shall bear fruit even in old age;
    vigorous and sturdy shall they be.

—Psalm 92:14-15, NAB

"Peace is what I leave with you, it is my own peace that I give you."

—John 14:27, TEV

Loving God,
all of us long for your peace.

Often we set out in search of it,
forgetting you have already given us this gift.

Give us light to reach down deep
into our own lives
to find where you have planted
your seeds of peace.

Give us courage
to nurture that peace and
to allow it to grow.

Teach us to be aware
of the seeds we must plant
in the lives of others.

And may the peace we live
give you praise and glory.

2. Time to Be Peaceful

In prayerful solitude I find not only God and myself but the world and all in it, not as it sees itself but as it stands in reality.

—Robert Faricy, S.J.

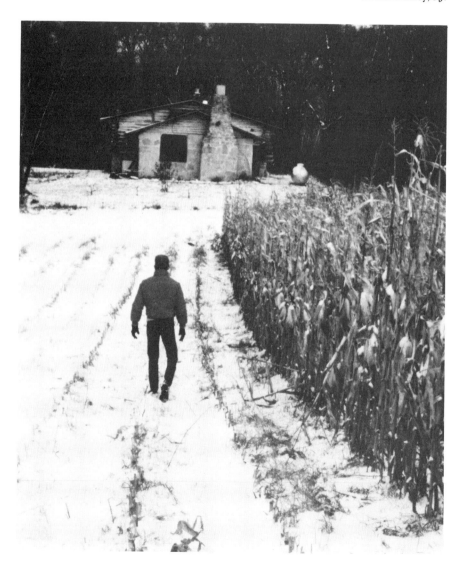

The Lord said,... "It is time for you to turn to me, your LORD, and I will come and pour out blessings upon you."

—Hosea 10:12, TEV

Jesus said to them, "Come by yourselves to an out-of-the-way place and rest a little."

—Mark 6:31, NAB

Where am I running to, Lord?
Why am I in such a hurry
when what I really want
is to slow down to your timing
and enjoy the present moment
you have given me?

Too often, when you give me
something to savor
I am mentally looking ahead
to what might happen next.

Slow me down, Lord:
my body,
my mind,
my reactions,
my emotions.
Get me off this racetrack.

Teach me how to go down deep
into the moment of now
to enjoy your goodness
in peace, with you.

3. Peace Begins in Me

It is in each of us that the peace of the world is cast... from there it must spread out to the limits of the universe.

—Leo Cardinal Suenens

The most important peace to have is peace within yourself. If you are at peace with yourself, you can spread it to others. If everyone would work toward having peace within themselves, we would have world peace. Since peace creates love and understanding, we would all basically get along. Because we're human we aren't all going to like each other, but if we can understand each other's differences and respect and love each other in spite of them, we can have peace.

—Michele E., grade 11

I wrestle often with the problem of peace in the world. Frequently, I'm tormented by the thought that I'm doing so little to bring about peace. It doesn't seem to be in my nature to march or carry signs. But I do try to bring peace to those around me wherever I go. My peace projects are very small ones. I just try to bridge gaps between people and to heal wounds in my own home, within our larger family of relatives, and in the various committees and groups I'm part of. Are these efforts successful? Outwardly, sometimes; inwardly, most of the time. I've learned to live with *trying.* I've learned to fault only my getting in God's way. I've learned not to give up on God and so not to give up on myself or others.

—Mary R., parent

Do you want long life and happiness? . . .
   strive for peace with all your heart.

—Psalm 34:12,14, TEV

The peace that Christ gives is to guide you in the decisions you make; for it is to this peace that God has called you together in the one body.

—Colossians 3:15, TEV

Lord, thank you
for giving me your peace.
Since I am your unique creation,
your peace in me will be unique.

When I am the best I can be,
centered in you,
your peace reigns in me
and naturally spreads
to those around me.

Help me to be open
more and more
to your call to peace.

Today I begin.

4. Leave Room for God to Work

All the good that you will do will come not from you but from the fact that you have allowed yourself, in the obedience of faith, to be used by God's love. Think of this more and gradually you will be free from the need to prove yourself, and you can be more open to the power that will work through you without your knowing it.

—Thomas Merton

A great example of peace in my life is when I accepted God as my leader. He takes over my life when I allow it, and has used me as his tool. In everything I do he guides me in peace, and I can depend on him for rest when I am uneasy.

—Melani D., grade 11

When I teach or give a talk, I write out only the bare outline so that there's room for the Holy Spirit to speak through me.

—Gertrude Foley, S.C., professor of theology

More and more, peace seems to me to be connected with acceptance: acceptance of my own limitations and gifts, acceptance of others just as they are, acceptance of circumstances beyond my control and situations I cannot change.

This kind of peace is very tied up with trust in God and his love for me and for all others. It has to do with a willingness to relinquish control and let God act instead of me. It is so much easier to be at peace with myself and others when I know and accept that God is in charge.

—Mary McF., parent

LORD,
　　everything that we achieve
　　is the result of what you do.

—Isaiah 26:12, TEV

To him who by means of his power working in us is able to do so much more than we can ever ask for, or even think of: to God be glory in the church and in Christ Jesus for all time, forever and ever! Amen.

—Ephesians 3:20, TEV

Lord God, why do we
take so much on ourselves
when you are waiting with your power
to work through us?

It's so easy to get in your way.
Teach us how to give you room.

Deliver us from limiting
what we might do for you
because we rely only on ourselves.

And thank you for always being there.
You are the Faithful One.

5. Will You Please Listen to Me?

*Listen to others talk. . . . You will probably be amazed to see
how often neither side listens actively to the other. . . . When
a child communicates, he wants concrete evidence that his
message has been received.*

—Dorothy Corkille Briggs

Dear Folks,

Thank you for everything, but I am going to Chicago to try and
start some kind of new life.

You asked me why I did those things and why I gave you so
much trouble, and the answer is easy for me to give you, but I am
wondering if you will understand.

Remember when I was about six or seven and I used to want you
to just listen to me? I remember all the nice things you gave me for
Christmas and my birthday and I was really happy with the things—
for about a week—at the time I got them. But during the rest of the
year I really didn't want presents. I just wanted you to listen to me
like I was somebody who felt things too, because I remember even
when I was young I felt things. But you said you were too busy.

Mom, you are a wonderful cook, and you had everything so
clean, and you were tired so much from doing all those things that
made you busy. But you know something, Mom? I would have liked
crackers and peanut butter just as well if you had only sat down with
me awhile during the day and said to me: "Tell me about it so I can
maybe help you understand."

And when Donna came I couldn't understand why everyone
made so much fuss, because I didn't think it was my fault that her hair
was curly and her skin so white, and she doesn't have to wear glasses
with such thick lenses. Her grades were better too, weren't they?

If Donna ever has children, I hope you will tell her to just pay
some attention to the one who doesn't smile very much because that
one will really be crying inside. And when she's about to bake six
dozen cookies, to make sure first that the kids don't want to tell her
about a dream or hope or something, because thoughts are important
to small kids too, even though they don't have so many words to use
when they tell about what they have inside them.

I think that all the kids who are doing so many things grown-ups are tearing their hair out worrying about are really looking for somebody that will have time to listen a few minutes and truly treat them as they would a grown-up who might be useful to them—you know, polite to them. If you folks ever said to me, "Pardon me," when you interrupted me, I'd have dropped dead!

If anybody asks you where I am, tell them I've gone looking for somebody with time because I've got a lot of things I want to talk about.

Love to all,
Your son
(a boy with a record
as a juvenile delinquent)

Happy is he who . . . speaks to attentive ears.

—Sirach 25:9, NAB

Jesus called for the children, saying: "Let the little children come to me. Do not shut them off. The reign of God belongs to such as these."

—Luke 18:16, NAB

**Loving God, thank you
for always being ready
to listen to me.
You are always there.**

**Forgive me for being so busy
that I often forget to listen,
especially to the children.**

**It's alarming to think that any of us
could be busy doing good things,
even great things,
and yet fail to listen to a child.**

**Teach me to listen
while there's still time.**

6. Before It's Too Late

History is replete with the bleached bones of nations that refused to listen to Jesus. May we in the twentieth century hear and follow his words—before it's too late.

—Martin Luther King, Jr.

He who closes his ear to the cry of the poor
will himself cry out and not be heard.

—Proverbs 21:13, RSV

The crowds asked him, "What ought we to do?" In reply Jesus said, "Let the man with two coats give to him who has none. The man who has food should do the same."

—Luke 3:10-11, NAB

Lord, have we refused to listen to you?
Are we, like the people of your own town,
deaf to your message, blind to your vision,
looking the other way when you carefully
point out the kingdom here, now?
Bleached bones! Lifeless, staring, empty, hopeless.
If I really let myself
take your words seriously,
that your kingdom is here in me right now,
I'd do something about it.
Maybe I think it's too good to be true.

Or maybe I'm afraid
to take it too seriously.
Afraid to accept such good news
for fear I'll have to give up something
if I go to an all-out belief.

Refusal to listen? Yes, Lord.
I think I'm guilty.
I know I'm guilty.
It's scary.

Do you actually want *me*
to do something about the condition of the world?
Me do something about your poor,
your homeless?
Me be a real live peacemaker?
Little me?
Why can't the ones with the power
do something about all these problems?
Why me?

Lord, don't you know I'm just beginning
to be comfortable?
If I really listen to you,
I'll definitely have to
make some changes.
And that's not comfortable.
Change often means pain.

But those bleached bones
staring at me,
asking why I didn't do something
when I had the chance.

Lord, I don't want my children
to see those bleached bones.
And I don't want my children to see me
pass them by
as if I had never noticed.

The children.
They mustn't *become* bleached bones
because I refused to listen
to your words.

Speak, Lord.
Really holler!
I'm ready to listen.

7. Facing Hunger

If the Christ of Scripture is our Lord, then we will refuse to be squeezed into the mold of our affluent, sinful culture.

—Ron Sider

After two thousand years of Christ's gospel of love, it's very sad to live in a world of hunger and poverty. Maybe it happens naturally as a result of the normal workings of social and economic systems we have constructed for ourselves. Also, because human beings are divided into rich and poor, it's hard for the poor to live a happy life. The rich control the lives of the poor, and our political system supports this. This causes the rich to get richer and the poor to get poorer.

We can't have a peaceful and prosperous world if a large part of the world's people are too near the edge of death because of hunger.

We all have a responsibility to work together to solve one of the greatest problems facing all nations today: world hunger. Hunger and famine must be stopped, and it's up to us. Our one hope is that the love and peace present in the people now helping the hungry and poor will forever continue flowing on to other people.

—Michael T., grade 10

Let justice roll down like waters,
    and righteousness like an everflowing stream.

—Amos 5:24, RSV

"Blessed are those who hunger
    and thirst for righteousness, for they shall be satisfied."

—Matthew 5:6, RSV

Loving God, I need your gift of courage
to take a real look
at the face of hunger
and not turn away.

How is it I have what I need
but others don't?

Don't let me accept poverty and hunger
because it's someone else's.

Stir up in me your own
thirst for justice
so that I will share
what I don't need
rather than waste it.

Enlighten me
so that I can look
with more honesty
at what I *think* I need.

8. Loving Our Neighbors: The Russians

What a privilege to have been brought to this point, to be the generation that saves God's creation and do what Jesus told us to do two thousand years ago.

—Dr. Helen Caldicott

Everyone seems to agree that in the long run the solution to our nuclear madness requires a change of heart, a conversion, a turning away from force and violence and a turning toward some form of global dispute settlement. An indispensable prerequisite to any such conversion is a change in the way Americans and Russians perceive each other. We must begin to see each other in a new light, freed from the fear and mistrust that have clouded our vision for so long.... What is needed is ... a willingness to confront the central and most difficult question: how am I to go about loving my neighbor, my enemy, the Russians? ... We need not wait for the Russians before beginning to transform ourselves. In the world of the mind and heart and spirit, we cannot wait, because we have been commanded by Christ to reach out to those who hate us. This is a unilateral and not a reciprocal obligation.

One way we can begin this conversion is to begin to know and understand the Russians. We must learn about Russia and its people. The statement may not be profound, but it is accurate: ignorance breeds distrust. We cannot love what we do not know. Just as we must spend time with our God if we wish our love to grow and our relationship to deepen, so we must spend time with Russian history, art, and literature if we are to forge a relationship of love.... What we seek is to separate the Soviet system of government, which we distrust, from the Russian people. We need to love the latter, not the former. Learning about the Russians is a way to pierce the Communist veil and see the human faces behind. People love and hate and work and play in Russia—people who are not very much different from us, people with dreams of a good life, peace, prosperity, and a better life for their children. These are the people we must love.

—Joseph Allegretti, professor of law

Here on Mount Zion the LORD Almighty will prepare a banquet for all the nations of the world—a banquet of the richest food and the finest wine. Here he will suddenly remove the cloud of sorrow that

has been hanging over all the nations. The Sovereign LORD will destroy death forever! He will wipe away the tears from everyone's eyes and take away the disgrace his people have suffered throughout the world. The LORD himself has spoken.

—Isaiah 25:6-8, TEV

But now in Christ Jesus you who once were far off have been brought near in the blood of Christ. For he is our peace, who has made us both one, and has broken down the dividing wall of hostility, by abolishing in his flesh the law of commandments and ordinances, that he might create in himself one new man in place of the two, so making peace, and might reconcile us both to God in one body through the cross, thereby bringing the hostility to an end.

—Ephesians 2:13-16, RSV

Lord, our God,
why do we waste so much time
building walls instead of bridges?
You've given us the challenge:
Love your neighbor as yourselves,
and love your enemies.
However we choose to look
at this problem,
you want us to love
the Russian people.
If we expect nothing but evil from them,
how will we ever recognize
the good they do?
Help us to put a face on these people
some call the enemy.
Give us the common sense
to separate a form of government
from men and women and children
who want a happy and peaceful life
just as much as we do.
Build your rainbow of peace
once again, Lord,
from one hemisphere to the other
so all your people and all creation
will live in harmony
praising you,
Yahweh, the Faithful One.

9. Tranquility Doesn't Mean Complacency

Come, Lord!
Do not smile and say
you are already with us.
Millions do not know you
and to us who do,
what is the difference?

What is the point
of your presence
if our lives do not alter?
Change our lives, shatter
our complacency.

Make your word
flesh of our flesh,
blood of our blood
and our life's purpose.
Take away the quietness
of a clear conscience.

Press us uncomfortably.
For only thus
that other peace is made,
your peace.

—Dom Helder Câmara

Like a moth drawn to the flame, I knew I'd end up reading the story I'd been avoiding for weeks. "The Last Testament" by Carol Amen is a fictional diary of herself and her children as they die from nuclear fall-out disease after a massive nuclear attack. I'd first seen it several months before in *MS* magazine and kept myself from reading it then. Now here it was again in the *Lutheran Standard.* I read. After all, it was only a hypothetical story. I felt sure I could handle that. But I wasn't able to. My grief was totally encompassing as I read. I was that mother watching her children die in her arms, helpless to save them or herself.

I ranted, I raved, I cried. I called out to God asking why. Why live, why raise children, why keep on working and building? Was there no future? I'd had such dreams for my two young sons—the kind of dreams that mothers live on. Were my dreams becoming nightmares? I loved my boys so. I couldn't bear to think of anything like this happening to them.

I wish I could say I suddenly came up with the magic answer. Nothing like that happened. But as the weeks and months went by, I found myself becoming calmer, finding hope in my faith that God means for us to continue living life to the fullest as long as we can, and wants us to do all we can to help make this world a better place for future generations.

In my own small way I've started along that path. I've joined the Women's International League for Peace and Freedom. I've helped sell their Stop the Arms Race buttons and handed out literature on the nuclear threat. I've put up bulletin boards at my church with a peace/anti-nuclear theme. It's not much, but I hope to continue doing what little I can.

But most importantly, I'll continue to build on my family's future. I refuse to give up on my hopes for my sons' lives. I'll do my best to help them grow up to be the caring, loving men we'll need in the peaceful world I've always dreamt of for them.

—Joan Brudahl Gale, parent

The LORD says, . . . "I alone know the plans I have for you, plans to bring you prosperity and not disaster, plans to bring about the future you hope for."

—Jeremiah 29:10-11, TEV

Through the Son, then, God decided to bring the whole universe back to himself. God made peace through his Son's death on the cross and so brought back to himself all things, both on earth and in heaven.

—Colossians 1:20, TEV

Lord, making peace is impossible
unless we take the message of your cross
into our own hearts
and make it part of our lives.
This may mean a change in our lives, Lord,
for your cross is disturbing.
If we allow ourselves to enter into
the message of your dying and rising,
we won't be able to be complacent
while there is hunger or poverty or
threat of destruction.
Bless us with the grace
of being disturbed.
Help us be unafraid
to alter our lives
through the cross of your peace.

10. Listening: The Beginning of Peace

We shall never truly know ourselves unless we find people who can listen, who can enable us to emerge, to come out of ourselves, to discover who we are. We cannot discover ourselves by ourselves.

—Edward Farrell

Silences.... For twenty years, our lives moved along filled with silences. Oh, we said "Good morning" and asked about the laundry to be done, what to serve for dinner, and we disciplined the children. But John and I never honestly talked to each other.

John was an alcoholic for most of our married life. I dealt with it as I had my parents' alcoholism . . . silently, as a long-suffering martyr.

At last I realized I had to get out if I was to survive.

Our divorce was civilized, just as our marriage had been. We made no great show of anger or any other emotion. I carefully kept all my resentments neatly tucked away.

Then John went into treatment and I went to Al-Anon. Slowly but surely, our lives began to change.

It began with phone calls from John. Sometimes several in a day; then I wouldn't hear from him for a week. But we talked about all sorts of things. At least John did.

I did a lot of listening. John obviously needed a friend to share his newfound ideas and feelings with. I knew that for the first time in his life, he was getting to know himself.

A new respect grew as we talked on the phone. One day he called me after I'd been sick for a week. I had had a bad time physically and emotionally.

We chatted a few minutes. Then he said, "You're better today."

"Yes," I replied. "My cold is much better."

"No, no, I don't mean that." He paused. "I mean you're better inside."

And he was right. Al-Anon was helping me put my life in order. I was learning to express what was going on inside me to a group of people who were truly listening to me. I was learning to "Let Go and Let God," and it felt very good.

During other phone conversations, we were each able to give something positive to the other. Freely given, gratefully accepted. I felt a great sense of peace. Listening had been the beginning of peace.

—Sally G., parent

"Will no one listen to what I am saying?" —Job 31:35, TEV

Remember this. . . . Everyone must be quick to listen, but slow to speak and slow to become angry.

—James 1:19, TEV

Loving Lord,
how do we learn to listen?
I want to be truly receptive
when another has a story to tell.
Give me a deep capacity
for hearing others as persons.
I know how it feels not to be heard, Lord.
I feel a tightening inside
when no one listens to me.

Help us to help
one another listen, Lord.
Open our ears,
our eyes,
our hearts.

11. What Can I Do?

*When he called his society together Jesus gave its members a
new way of life to live. He gave them a new way to deal with
offenders—by forgiving them. He gave them a new way to
deal with violence—by sharing it. He gave them a new way
to deal with the problems of leadership—by drawing upon
the gift of every member, even the most humble. He gave
them a new way to deal with corrupt society—by building a
new order, not smashing the old.*

—John Howard Yoder

Each person can do something constructive to take meaningful, effective steps toward a more peaceful world. Each must look to his own conscience to discover what he should do to promote peace. Suggestions like the following may be of some assistance:

1. *Learn about peace.* It is harder to work for peace than to drift into war. Keep informed about current events and examine the various proposals advanced for the achieving of a peaceful world.

2. *Promote peace through education.* A "peace" dimension can be added to almost any course of study from grade school through university. The humanities can focus on the religious, social, and historical views of peace. The sciences can examine man's technological achievements and what these can do to remove the seeds of global war. Business subjects can discuss the role of business in shaping a world free from want.

3. *Break the link between violence and courage.* The man or woman of moral strength is the one who energetically labors for non-violent solutions to community and national problems. Courage and violence have no necessary connection.

4. *Puncture the myth.* Convince others that war is neither noble nor glorious. Total war, in this nuclear age, is an unspeakable evil, universally condemned by thinking men of every faith and conviction.

5. *Shape public opinion.* Through everyday conversations, letters to newspapers and your elected representatives, you can help dispose countless persons towards peace and away from war.

6. *Cooperate with others.* Associate yourself with responsible individuals and groups to call for such programs as economic assistance to needy countries . . . limitation of the arms race . . . a cabinet-level Department of Peace . . . provision of selective conscientious objectors.

7. *Vote for peace.* Become involved in party politics to participate in the selection of primary candidates who are peace-minded rather

than war-minded. Take the time and trouble to secure their election and back them up when their advocacy of peace leads them into taking unpopular positions.

8. *Support the United Nations.* With all its handicaps, the United Nations provides a forum for the peaceful airing of disputes, furnishes a peace-keeping force to police contested borders and recruits technical experts to promote human betterment in economically underdeveloped regions.

9. *Encourage true patriotism.* The real patriot is the person who is not afraid to criticize the defective policies of the country which he loves. He never belittles or disdains the affection of others for their native lands. Our common humanity is more basic than any political distinctions.

—Joseph J. Fahey, Manhattan College

In days to come,
The mountains of the LORD's house
    shall be established as the highest mountain
    and raised above the hills.
All nations shall stream toward it. . . .
He shall judge between the nations,
    and impose terms on many peoples.
They shall beat their swords into plowshares
    and their spears into pruning hooks;
One nation shall not raise the sword against another,
    nor shall they train for war again.   —Isaiah 2:2,4, NAB

When anyone is joined to Christ, he is a new being; the old is gone, the new has come. All this is done by God, who through Christ changed us from enemies into his friends and gave us the task of making others his friends also.

—2 Corinthians 5:17-18, TEV

Lord Jesus,
you've given us a whole new way to live,
but it's a lesson we're slow to learn.

Through the example of your life
and the reality of your grace
we have within us the power
to bring peace to this world.

We ask you now for courage
to look honestly into our consciences
to see what we can do for peace.

We've created the problems.
With your help we can solve them.

12. Prayer: The Heart of Peace

After looking at the lives of many peacemakers and trying to understand what kept them going, it seems to me that the only thing that will sustain us to be peacemakers throughout our lives is prayer. . . . The more central prayer becomes to our life as peacemakers, the longer we will be able to act as children of God. For blessed are the peacemakers, they shall be called sons and daughters of God.

—Chuck Walters

"Let us pray now for those mourning the death of loved ones. . . ." This was the pastor's bidding prayer, followed by a time of silence. I was worshiping on a Sunday morning, coincidentally my birthday.

Then, to my great surprise, I found myself praying for Mrs. Leonid Brezhnev, widow of the Soviet leader who had died the week before. Viktoria Brezhnev—a woman mourning the death of her husband of many years, a grandmother, a great-grandmother.

Why did I feel so strange praying for Mrs. Brezhnev? I pray for others I don't know by name, others whose faces I have never seen, others who live far from my home.

I pride myself on being a Christian, on being open-minded, on being one who wants and works for peace. Yet it seemed peculiar to me—almost a bit embarrassing—to be praying for Mrs. Brezhnev. After all, she is a Communist, or at least is married to one, or her husband led a world power in rivalry with the nation where I make my home.

"Be constant in prayer. . . . Bless those who persecute you. . . . Weep with those who weep. . . . If possible, so far as it depends upon you, live peaceably with all . . ." (Romans 12:12,14,15,18 RSV).

So I see that the roots of war are in me, too—an insight from my own prayer, perhaps God's birthday gift to me this year.

—Hermann Weinlick, parent

Be still, and know that I am God.   —Psalm 46:10, RSV

We ask God to fill you with the knowledge of his will, with all the wisdom and understanding that his Spirit gives. Then you will be able to live as the Lord wants and will always do what pleases him. Your lives will produce all kinds of good deeds, and you will grow in your knowledge of God.

—Colossians 1:9-10, TEV

Lord, teach us how to pray.
Our peacemaking won't be authentic
unless it begins and ends
in you.

There's a busy part of us
that urges us to be always out doing something.
But you've told us that being quiet with you
is essential too.

How can we know what you want us to do
if we don't take time out to communicate with you?

Help us not to be afraid
of what we might learn
if we are still.

Let our lives be a work of peace
because we have discovered
you
and ourselves in you.

13. Jesus: The Active Listener

Christ's existence was ruled by a great silence. His soul was listening. It was given over to the needs of others. . . . He was unreservedly receptive.

—Ladislaus Boros

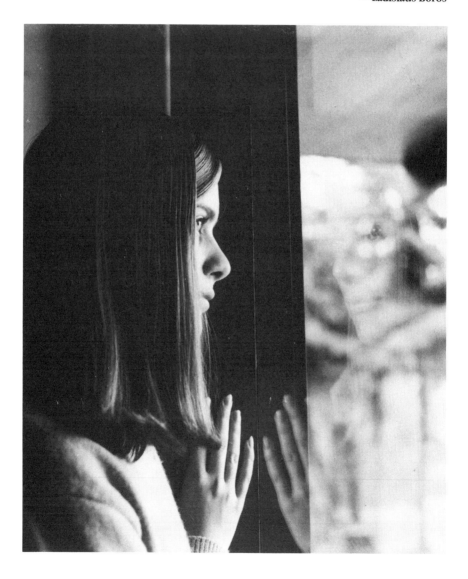

The Sovereign LORD has taught me what to say,
　　so that I can strengthen the weary.
Every morning he makes me eager
　　to hear what he is going to teach me.
The LORD has given me understanding,
　　and I have not rebelled
　　or turned away from him.　　　　　　　—Isaiah 50:4-5, TEV

The one whom God has sent speaks God's words, because God gives
him the fullness of his Spirit.

　　　　　　　　　　　　　　　　　　　—John 3:34, TEV

Jesus, you are the example we need.
You have taught us that
in order to communicate well
we have to learn to listen.
In the Gospels
every word you spoke
was just what was needed.
It is impossible to imagine you
wasting words.
You knew what to say to those around you
because you listened with all your attention,
just as you listened to the Father.

Were you able to be attentive to others
because you were so open to God?

Please help me learn to listen
so that my words, like yours,
will be just what is needed.

IMAGES
OF
PEACE

As we listen and think about peace, we begin to talk about it with words of peace; with words that forgive and are not judgmental; with words of cheer and humor; with words that are sensitive to the feelings of others; with words that encourage and inspire and affirm. We become more peace-conscious, and we find peace and courage in reaching out to others peacefully and with courage.

Part Two
Speak Peace to One Another

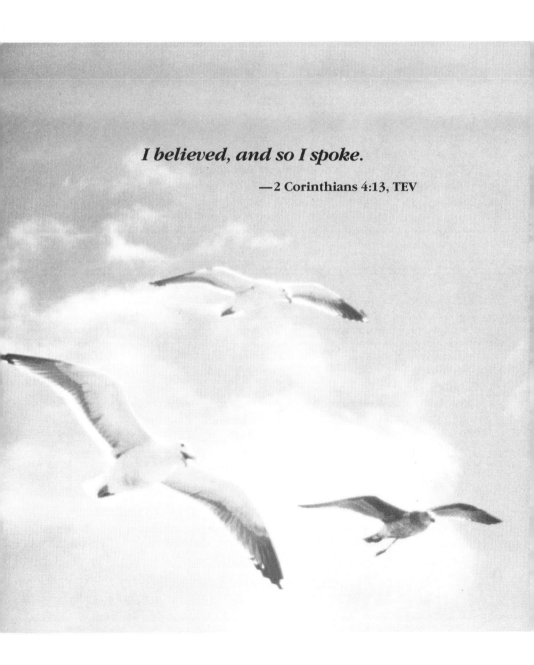

I believed, and so I spoke.

—2 Corinthians 4:13, TEV

14. A Need to Forgive and Be Forgiven

We must be saved by the final form of love which is forgiveness.

—Reinhold Niebuhr

An example of peacemaking could be just saying "I'm sorry." But for me to say that isn't enough. I feel I need to change what I'm doing, and the way I change is a concrete way of peacemaking. For instance, there was a time when I put my parents through a lot of heartaches. Then something happened that made me see what I was doing. Saying I'm sorry wouldn't have been enough, so I not only said it but changed what I was doing that was hurting them so much.

—Barb H., grade 12

I've lived in this nursing home for eleven years. I lived through the Great Depression and other hard times, and two wars. The only way to have peace is to be reconciled to God and to one another and to pray daily. Do it now before it's too late. Do as Jesus said: "Love one another as I have loved you."

—Mayme K., nursing-home resident

In spite of all our desire for reconciliation, there will be times when peacemaking is one-sided. There are words of peace that we will never speak, and words of peace that we will never hear, either because the opportunity is past or because human limitations are too great. But healing, if not reconciliation, must take place somehow if we are to go on as whole and healthy people.

Is one-sided peace possible? It is if we realize there are times when peace no longer depends on our actions and that we cannot control the actions of others. We are responsible for doing all the good we can, because hostility may ultimately be overcome with good, but never with hostility. Once we've done all we can, we leave the peacemaking to God. Leaving it to him may mean accepting brokenness, because it is part of life. But beyond this, if we are willing to trust God, he can heal the painful memories we are left with. He can also, in his own time, change the hearts of people in ways that we cannot imagine or foresee. For our own healing, we must be willing to let go of hate, of hurt, but never of hope.

—Lyn Klug, parent

"Do not bear a grudge against anyone, but settle your differences. . . ."

—Leviticus 19:17, TEV

Do everything possible on your part to live in peace with everybody.

—Romans 12:18, TEV

Forgiving Lord, you are so patient with us.
Some lessons we have to learn
over and over,
and forgiveness is one of them.
We often forget your words and example,
and when we leave you out of our lives
we find it hard to forgive.
Teach us today
how much we need to be forgiven
so we'll be more ready to forgive.
Help us to allow you
to touch us
so that when we forgive
we rebuild what was broken
with love.

15. Please Encourage Me

We are one, after all, you and I; together we suffer, together exist, and forever will recreate each other.

—Teilhard de Chardin

As a special project in our high school, a group of teachers were trying to help our young people realize that they are a gift, . . . a gift to themselves and a gift to others from God. To help point out their individual "giftedness," I asked each of their parents to write a letter to their son or daughter just letting them know how much they think of them. On a retreat weekend, before the closing prayer service on Friday evening, I passed out the letters to my group. There wasn't a sound in the room lit by fireplace and candles as each read things that aren't said often enough, or perhaps are never said at all.

After commenting briefly on the letters, I gave the group a short break. I walked outside and said a special prayer of thanks for the parents who had written their kids and for the response it had brought about. As I was about to go back into the building, Tom said he had to show me something. Now, Tom was a sophomore, and to many people he may have seemed a little wild at times. The Tom I knew, though, was a very sensitive guy who cared a great deal about others, and who wanted desperately to be involved in helping them. I followed him out to the edge of the path, and as he turned, I saw that he was crying. He said, "That letter—that was the best. My folks have never said those things to me before. I guess they can't. It was sure nice to hear they're proud of me. I've always been compared to my older brother. He's real smart and everything, and I'm just not good at that stuff. People are always telling me what I'm not good at. I was just sitting down by the lake during the break."

He leaned forward and started to get very excited. "I had this flashlight, and I was just about ready to come back in when I shined the light up into the trees. I saw all the leaves on this one branch. All of them were different, but they were on the same branch. I figured, if they can be different, so can I, and for the first time I started thinking about the things I'm really good at!"

He started to cry a little more, and since my philosophy has always been to give a hug when words fall short, that's exactly what I did. For the first time, Tom was beginning to see his true giftedness. The hurt he had felt for so long had been healed.

—Mike Jeremiah, high-school campus minister

Encourage: To inspire to continue on a chosen course; impart courage or confidence to; embolden; hearten.

—*American Heritage Dictionary*

Worry can rob you of happiness, but kind words will cheer you up.

—**Proverbs 12:25, TEV**

Encourage one another. Live in harmony and peace, and the God of love and peace will be with you.

—**2 Corinthians 13:11, NAB**

Lord,
how quickly we would spread peace
if we took the time
to always be encouraging.
Encouragement builds up
as surely as negativism breaks down.
We are all in this together,
and we need to tell one another we are okay.
Open our eyes to see what is good
and growing and life-giving
in ourselves and in others.
Lord, en-courage us in this special way
of loving.

16. The Healing Power of Kids

We believe in children: little ones, big ones, and chubby ones. There is faith in their eyes, love in their touch, hope in their attitude. We thrill with them at life's joys, bow with them in worship, and hold them close in tragedy. We believe in children: the fragile dreams of yesterday, life's radiant reality today, and vibrant substance of tomorrow. We believe in children, for wherever we go we find yesterday's children who were nurtured in love, truth, and beauty at work trying to make this world a better place for everyone.

—Anonymous

Often we hear "Children and teenagers are so selfish these days. One wonders what will become of them." I don't know about all of them, but I have had contact with about 250 of them here in our parish this past week. Did you know that about twenty-five high-school and college kids went caroling to our homebound, made them cards, and brought them each a rose? All their own idea.

Our grade-school children made cards and door decorations, caroled, made gifts for those at nearby nursing homes and for our parishioners who were unable to leave their homes.

Yes, you do wonder what will become of them! I for one am glad the future is in their hands.

—Patrice Neuberger, C.S.J., parish minister

Many grade schools and high schools have become involved with caring for the elderly in neighborhood nursing homes and high-rises. One school in particular matches up each child with a senior citizen in September. The children, with the help of their teachers, are responsible for sending greetings and other signs of caring to "their people" as often as they wish, but especially at holidays.

A group of second graders were given names of a couple who had been housebound for a long time. The husband was confined to a wheel chair, and his wife cared for him constantly. Neither had been out of the house for many months when the children started visiting them. The couple looked forward to their visits and always tried to have a treat ready when they stopped by on Friday afternoons.

The love and attention of these children worked its own magic.

Recently, the couple celebrated their twenty-fifth wedding anniversary and decided to share with their friends in second grade a gift they had received. One day the couple appeared in the doorway of the second-grade classroom, beaming and waiting expectantly. The teacher called the small group of children forward. They were amazed that the couple could even get out of their house, but the real surprise was handed them in an envelope—a check for fifty dollars.

"You kids have been so thoughtful for such a long time. Now we want to do something for you. We want your whole class to have a nice party."

—PCH

Children are a gift from the LORD,
    they are a real blessing.

—Psalm 127:3, TEV

Since you are God's dear children, you must try to be like him. Your life must be controlled by love, just as Christ loved us and gave his life for us.

—Ephesians 5:1,2, TEV

God, thank you for the special gift of love
you have given us in young people.
They are a fresh reflection of you:
creative and abounding in life.

Did you bless them
with insatiable curiosity
and unending questions
to keep those of us who are called
"experienced"
young and full of wonder?

Teach us how to listen to them,
to learn from them and value them,
and especially to love them.

We thank you and praise you
that your kingdom belongs to them.

17. Give Them Roses
While They're Still Living

Our first question is not how to go out and help the elderly, but how to allow the elderly to enter into the center of our own lives, how to create the space where they can be heard and listened to from within with careful attention.

—Henri Nouwen

Dear Abby: Recently I lost my dear mother, who was eighty-five. The next few days I was kept busy entertaining relatives and friends who came to cry. Most of them had not seen Mother in twenty-five years or more.

Later as they were leaving, the tears reappeared along with the same utterances from each, "I hope next time we will meet it will be for a happier occasion."

Abby, where were those criers when Mother spent her last four years in a nursing home waiting for someone to come and visit her?

—"Dear Abby" column

Dear Lord,
my fire burns warm
against the wintry night.
The old clock ticks away
the hours.
Gently falling snow
mutes the noisy street.

In my hand is the Book
to bring me comfort
in my solitude.

Yet I'm lonely,
not because I'm alone
but because I'm not expecting
anyone.
There is no one to come.

Dear Father of us all,
bring me inner peace.

—Edith McN., age 94,
nursing-home resident

Cast me not off in my old age;
as my strength fails, forsake me not.
—Psalm 71:9, NAB

Jesus said to his mother, "Woman, there is your son." In turn he said to the disciple, "There is your mother." From that hour onward, the disciple took her into his care.
—John 19:26-27, NAB

Lord Jesus,
sometimes my life is so full,
so busy and preoccupied,
I forget there are many
for whom the days are long and lonely.
At this time in my life
it's hard to imagine
what it would be like
to be old
or neglected
or without a friend.
I know how important these older folks
are to you, Lord.
Show me how to make them feel
important and valuable,
how to let them be
at the center of my life,
not out on the fringes.
Give me the good sense
to learn from their wisdom and experience.
Bless them, Lord,
and keep them in your peace.

18. In Giving We Receive

I am only one,
But still I am one.
I cannot do everything,
But still I can do something;
And because I cannot do everything
I will not refuse to do the something that I can do.

—Edward Everett Hale

Several years ago God offered us a precious gift that my husband and I almost turned down. One weekend in the fall a friend asked, "Ceil, an Ethiopian young woman is here for open-heart surgery. Do you know someone who would take her in?"

I promised to ask around. It seemed everyone was as busy as we were. Then it hit me. We were like the innkeeper—no room at the inn. Couldn't we squeeze a stranger in somewhere?

We said yes. And Sarah, with shining black eyes and hair braided like a crown on her head, moved into our lives and hearts.

Two weeks later, I stood by her side in Intensive Care. Hooked into tubes, she looked like a fragile child. Her eyes fluttered open. She smiled. Joy flooded me as I realized I was the link between her parents, an ocean away, and Sarah, God's special gift to us.

Sarah, now restored to health, is in her senior year of college and happily married. Her sister Azeb is here now and also calls us Mom and Dad.

Two years ago Hare, needing ear surgery, flew in from Ethiopia with her older sister. We had to put our trust in God to meet their needs: with health, school, visas. What joy to receive God's answers: a four-year college scholarship for the older sister, medical expenses paid by the Crippled Children's Fund, and refugee status with work permits secured.

From war-torn Ethiopia young people flock to America today and discover peace and freedom. For substitute parents like ourselves, they are God's gifts of joy.

—Ceil McLeod, parent

"The sojourner, the fatherless, and the widow, who are within your towns, shall come and eat and be filled; that the LORD your God may bless you in all the work of your hands that you do."

—Deuteronomy 14:29, RSV

The Spirit we have received is not the world's spirit but God's Spirit, helping us to recognize the gifts he has given us.

—Corinthians 2:12, NAB

Loving God,
you are so good to us.
Every day you send us your gifts
in the form of friends and strangers,
sometimes in problems and often in joys.
You offer us challenges;
sometimes even failure is a gift.

Help us to keep alert to your presence
in our lives, Lord.
Teach us to welcome you
in whatever way you choose to come.

19. Taking a Closer Look

A Christian fellowship lives and exists by the intercession of its members for one another, or it collapses. I can no longer condemn or hate a brother for whom I pray, no matter how much trouble he causes me. His face, that hitherto may have been strange and intolerable to me, is transformed in intercession into the countenance of a brother for whom Christ died, the face of a forgiven sinner.

—Dietrich Bonhoeffer

Peace is finding the good about people and nature and showing how good these people and things really are. It is getting along with the world, no matter how much confrontation there is. We can still find peace.

Once on a school retreat I met a lot of people I didn't know well in school. In the past I had judged them harshly. Through lots of discussion sessions and prayer services I got to know these people and found they were so good inside. This taught me how important it is to get to know people, even ones you might not like, and especially not to judge them.

—Sue P., grade 11

The kind of peace Jesus preached had to do with breaking down barriers, inner and outer.... The barriers in the outer world between different kinds of people and between people of different kinds of beliefs and meaning systems will break down only when those walls built against our own rejected parts are broken open. This breaking open, this carrying of our cross, this dying to ourselves, allows us to see our oneness with the fragile beauty of every living being; harshness and hatred are destroyed. Herein lies the peace that Jesus wishes us; this is the peace that creates peace outside of ourselves.

The path to breaking down of inner barriers is a narrow path, not heavily populated. The path is one of prayer and solitude—not the prayer and solitude of willpower, but the prayer and solitude of nakedness before our whole selves in the light God calls us to: "The one who lives by the truth comes into the light."

—Patricia Keefe, O.S.F.

Create a pure heart in me, O God,
      and put a new and loyal spirit in me.   —Psalm 51:6,10, TEV

"Do not judge others, so that God will not judge you, for God will judge you in the same way you judge others, and he will apply to you the same rules you apply to others."

—Matthew 7:1-2, TEV

Lord, you said we should
love our enemies and
pray for those who bother us,
and you showed us how to do that.
But it's so hard to do.
It means that no matter what happens
I must respond with love,
with peace.
It means that I must look
more honestly at myself
and take others as they are
without passing judgment.
It means I must try to bridge gaps
and break down barriers
rather than create them.
Teach me to see the good in others
through my prayer for them.
Give me an understanding heart
that is loving enough
to transform one whom
I thought to be an enemy
into a friend.

20. Peacemaking Requires Lots of Love

Your children are not your children.
They are the sons and daughters of Life's longing for itself.
They come through you but not from you,
And though they are with you yet they belong not to you.
You may give them your love but not your thoughts,
For they have their own thoughts. . . .
You may strive to be like them, but seek not to make them
like you.

—Kahlil Gibran

My example of peacemaking involves two people I feel very close to. One is a man named Joseph. When Joseph was a child, he was very poor but happy. As he grew up he worked very hard and lived comfortably. He married and had a son named Mark. Joseph was very happy. Never before was there a father so devoted to his son. Joseph loved Mark so much. He wanted Mark to have everything he had never had. He didn't want Mark to make the same mistakes he had made.

However, Joseph didn't understand that Mark had to live his own life and make his own decisions. Instead of offering his experience and helpful advice, Joseph simply told Mark what to do. Joseph tried to make Mark's decisions about career, life-style, education, and morality. But Mark, who had his own ideas, rebelled. That so enraged Joseph that he called Mark "good for nothing" and "ungrateful" and kicked him out of the house.

Joseph simply didn't realize that he was being unfair. He truly believed he was right. He did it all out of his strong love for Mark. He wanted to teach Mark a lesson. He thought that Mark would realize that his father was right all along and come home.

But something quite different happened. It took Mark a long time and a lot of hard work, but he made it through college and got a job he really enjoyed. It was not the kind of job that Joseph had wanted for him, but it was what Mark wanted for himself. It hurt Mark a lot, though, that he couldn't communicate with his father anymore. Even more, it hurt Joseph to know he had lost his son. He loved his son.

The day Joseph turned sixty, he realized that nothing should be important enough to harm his relationship with his only son. He felt very awkward, but he called Mark, tried to speak, and began to cry. Mark understood. He wished his father a happy birthday. It was the best birthday present Joseph had ever received: the return of his son. Joseph realized he had been stubborn and one-sided. The love these two people shared was what restored peace to their relationship.

—Joanne T., grade 11

The LORD gave us mind and conscience; we cannot hide from ourselves.

—Proverbs 20:27, TEV

"His father ran, threw his arms around his son, and kissed him."

—Luke 15:20, TEV

Loving God, thank you
for the gift of our children.
Sometimes we have such high hopes
of our own for them
we forget to let them
be themselves.

Give us wisdom and love
to cherish who they are
and who they can become.

Give our children
wisdom and love
to be the best they can be.

21. Bearing One Another's Burdens: Peer Ministry

A true Christian is a sign of contradiction—a living symbol of the Cross. He or she is a person who believes the unbelievable, bears the unbearable, forgives the unforgivable, loves the unlovable, is perfectly happy not to be perfect, is willing to give up his or her will, becomes weak to be strong, sees some good in every bad and finds love by giving it away. A Christian transcends the natural with the immeasurable power of love and becomes a supernatural person.

—Joseph Roy

As a campus minister in a suburban high school, I am concerned that so many young people these days have enormous problems to face and solve. To meet this need, we have developed a special program called Peer Ministry in which kids learn to take the time to reach out to other kids who are suffering. Retreat time frequently provides the time and place for this reaching out. On a particular Friday evening, we were preparing for a one-on-one, a time when they are given a specific topic or goal to accomplish and are given the chance to pick one person to spend the time with in talking or working on the particular area. That night's topic was forgiveness—of self and of others.

One of the seniors there was a boy named Jim. He was really down on himself. He hadn't been very successful in relationships, especially with girls, and Chris, the girl he had been dating, had just told him she didn't think it was a good idea for them to go out any longer. Chris tried to explain that she wanted to date other boys, but Jim refused to listen. Chris told me Jim even refused to acknowledge her presence and said he would have nothing to do with her or with any of his old friends. It was as though he had crawled into his shell.

During the one-on-one time, I walked around the camp noticing people busily talking—on the assigned topic, I hoped. I saw Jim sitting in front of the fireplace with Paul, a member of our Peer Ministry group at school. I prayed that Paul might be able to get through to Jim where we adults hadn't been so successful. As the hour ended, the kids returned to the main meeting room and began sharing things from their one-on-ones.

As always, I was most impressed with the openness and honesty of these kids. At one point in the sharing, there was a brief pause that was soon broken as Jim and Paul stood up. Paul began by saying that he had spent his one-on-one with Jim and that he had gotten a lot out of it. Jim broke in at this point and said that he was the one who had gotten the most out of it. He said that he had been acting really dumb for the past few weeks, shutting himself off from everyone and feeling sorry for himself. He apologized openly to his friends for this and said a special "I'm sorry" to Chris for not listening or trying to understand. Chris got up from her seat across the room and gave Jim and Paul a big hug. Everyone applauded.

Later that night, I asked Paul what he had said to Jim to make such a difference. He said he had shared some of the times when he himself had been hurt and how he felt at those times; how he too felt like locking himself away from everyone but how that really wouldn't be living. Finally, Paul said the secret words: "I don't think I said anything different from anyone else. I think Jim was just ready to hear."

That night as we closed with our evening prayer, I said a special prayer of thanks to God for touching us so beautifully. I prayed that more people in our world might be open to that touch, seeing themselves as instruments of his healing in their lives and the lives of others.

—Mike J., campus minister

The Lord will make you go through hard times, but he himself will be there to teach you, and you will not have to search for him any more.

—Isaiah 30:20, TEV

Help carry one another's burdens, and in this way you will obey the law of Christ.

—Galatians 6:2, TEV

**Lord Jesus, thank you
for giving us one another.
You never said that
following you would be easy,
but you've given us yourself
and you've given us one another
for support along the way.
Help us to be open enough
to give or receive that help.
Teach us to bring out peace
in one another.
Teach us to *be* peace
to one another.**

22. Laughter: The Great Healer

Joy is the most infallible sign of the presence of God.

—Leon Bloy

Peggy Williams is a clown.

The first female graduate of the Ringling Brothers and Barnum and Bailey Clown College in Florida, she spends her life making people happy.

"Laughter seems to draw us together," she says. "It's one thing that automatically can jump across all boundaries that we set up by verbal language."

As a clown, she's found a universal form of communication. "Laughter," she says, "transcends everything and makes you feel good."

—*Christopher News Notes*

I made the joyous discovery that ten minutes of genuine belly laughter had an anesthetic effect and would give me at least two hours of pain-free sleep. . . . Some people, in the grip of uncontrollable laughter, say their ribs are hurting. The expression is probably accurate, but it is a delightful "hurt" that leaves the individual relaxed almost to the point of an open sprawl. It is the kind of "pain" too, that most people would do well to experience every day of their lives. It is as specific and tangible as any other form of physical exercise. . . . Long before my own serious illness, I became convinced that creativity, the will to live, faith, hope, and love have biochemical significance and contribute strongly to healing and well-being. The positive emotions are life-giving experiences. . . . Scientific research has established the existence of endorphins in the human brain—a substance very much like morphine in its molecular structure and effects. It is the body's own anesthesia and a relaxant and helps human beings to sustain pain. . . . Enough research has been done to indicate that those individuals with determination to overcome an illness tend to have a greater tolerance to severe pain than those who are morbidly apprehensive. . . .

—Norman Cousins

A cheerful heart is a good medicine,
but a downcast spirit dries up the bones. —Proverbs 17:22, RSV

May the God of hope fill you with all joy and peace in believing, so
that by the power of the Holy Spirit you may abound in hope.

—Romans 15:13, RSV

God of joy, thank you for the gift
of a good laugh.
Like music and love,
it speaks all languages
and has a healing power
all its own.

Help us to remember
there is nothing life-giving
about being gloomy.

Let our belief in you
and our trust in your care
be so complete
that our joy will be the sure sign
of your presence
in this world
that needs you so much.

23. Harmony of Young and Old

Age is opportunity no less
Than youth itself, though in another dress
And as the evening twilight fades away,
The sky is filled with stars invisible by day.

—Henry Wadsworth Longfellow

A special project in Minneapolis combines a nursing home and day-care center that allows for easy mingling of babies and "instant grandparents." On their way to work, the mothers leave their small ones (under the age of fifteen months) in the Oak and Acorn Nursery, which is several rooms in the lower level of the home. This area was recently redecorated and furnished with rocking chairs, cribs, toys, blankets, diapers, and a small kitchen where a few of the residents sometimes bake cookies or other goodies while their small friends nap. Baby food and bottles are also warmed there. Under the supervision of day-care specialists, the babies keep the interested residents active and alert and feeling needed, while the babies enjoy a hug, a lap, and lots of smiles and touches.

Martha, a resident in her late seventies, seemed to sum up the feeling shared by all. We watched her rock a little one slowly back and forth. The expression on her face was euphoric as the baby looked right into her eyes, cooed, and reached out to touch her cheek. Martha said softly, "This is a dream come true for me. You see, I've never had any grandchildren of my own."

—PCH

Arlene Symons of Brooklyn, New York, has discovered an effective way for young and old to relate to one another—through projects of mutual interest.

After years of teaching children, Mrs. Symons branched out to working with senior citizen centers by developing choral groups. But most of the time she noticed that the elderly people performed primarily before other elderly people. "Where are their children and grandchildren?" she wondered. Often the children were similarly isolated from other age groups.

Mrs. Symons later went back to teaching music in elementary school, but she held on to one chorus of elderly people. Gradually she developed an idea for ending the isolation of the elderly. In the school, she rehearsed her group of 100 nine- and ten-year-olds. In a separate location she rehearsed her group of the elderly. For a period of about three and a half months she got the two groups writing back and forth, pen-pal fashion. Mrs. Symons called it the thread that held the program together. Through the letters, relationships grew as the pen pals learned about each other's life-style. During the final week before the concert, the children joined the older adults for music rehearsals at the center. The young and old pen pals gathered for lunch—and talked.

"We put the right people together," one said. "What has happened is that they have experienced something that has changed their lives. It's natural; it's life."

—*Media Tip Sheet*

"I have loved you with an everlasting love;
    therefore I have continued my faithfulness to you."

—Jeremiah 31:3, RSV

Each one, as a good manager of God's different gifts, must use for the good of others the special gift he has received from God.

—1 Peter 4:10, TEV

Lord, our God,
you have made us all unique,
with special gifts to share
at every stage of our lives.
We thank you especially
for the bond you have created
between the very young
and the very old.
The love they have to offer each other
is inspiring to see
and enriches us all.
Let their love
help us to be more and more aware
of the need all ages have
for a hug, a kind word, a touch.

24. Choosing Peace as a Goal

Peacemaking is fundamentally a spiritual struggle, a battle for the soul of humanity.

—Richard Barnet, a founder of World Peacemakers

We are witnessing the beginnings of a conversion in the churches—a conversion to peace. The signs of it are everywhere. It is a movement of faith and conscience, not just a political phenomenon. Where the commitment to peace is emerging, so is Bible study, prayer, the renewal of worship, and community.

The new Christian peace movement is taking hold at the local level and is deeply ecumenical. Catholics are working beside Mennonites, evangelicals, and mainline Protestants. The urgent matter of peace has the ability to unite the denominations more than anything has in years. It is increasingly important that this unity of Christian conscience be demonstrated publicly.

The prospect of many Christians and their churches turning toward peace would certainly pose a powerful political challenge to current government policies. A great opportunity for collective Christian witness is emerging. The convergence of a number of significant events and plans suggests that some Spirit is afoot.

—Jim Wallis

Anyone you ask is likely to affirm a desire for "peace on earth." Most will even tell you that they pray for peace. Here are some statistics on persons who are affiliated with religions which believe in peace, justice, and world order:

- More than one billion Christians and Jews profess "Thou shalt not kill" as one of their Ten Commandments.
- Some 460 million Moslems believe that "islam" means "peace through submission to God."
- Another 416 million Hindus believe that all creatures have a soul and must be treated with reverence. They seek unity with the entire universe.
- Confucius' followers, numbering 300 million, trust that by obedience in human relationships they will achieve the harmony and justice planned by heaven.
- Some 200 million Buddhists seek Nirvana, the state of complete peace and love.

- About 300 million Taoists find harmony in simplicity and humility, evidenced in kindness to all persons and things.

Those who profess peace as their goal are united with nearly 2.5 billion others whose religions stress love, reverence for life, justice, and peace. Added to these are the millions more whose quest for peace is prompted by ethical or humanist motives. Imagine a world in which all of us who "speak peace" pursue peace by making it a goal worthy of our time and talents.

—The Christophers' *Peace Packet*

"Today I am giving you a choice between good and evil, between life and death. . . . Choose life. Love the LORD your God, obey him and be faithful to him, and then you and your descendants will live long in the land. . . ."

—Deuteronomy 30:15,19-20, TEV

Try to be at peace with everyone, and try to live a holy life, because no one will see the Lord without it.

—Hebrews 12:14, TEV

Lord, our God,
what a world this would be
if we all actively pursued peace!
You have planted the longing for peace
because we live in such a hurry,
too busy attaining things
to provide a quiet space
for peace to develop?

We *need* a conversion, Lord.
We need to return to our own
deepest longings.
We need to put our actions
where our speeches are
and to pursue peace
with all our time and talents.

Engrave in our minds and hearts
such a vision of this world at peace
that it will empower us
to make it a reality.

Let us feel your presence,
God of peace.
We need you.

25. Peace, Like Love, Begins at Home

Communication is the most important element of family life because it is basic to loving relationships. It is the energy that fuels the caring, giving, sharing, and affirming. Without genuine sharing of ourselves, we cannot know one another's needs and fears. Good communication is what makes all the rest of it work.

—Dolores Curran

I think peace is getting along with yourself and everybody around you, helping each other out in time of need. We make peace in our family when we all sit down and talk out our family problems. My brother and I helped talk our parents out of a divorce.

—Mike K., grade 11

Peace has to begin with those closest to you, and sometimes that's very hard. Just a while ago, my brother and I had many problems getting along. Ever since we were little kids, we had never gotten along very well. Either we fought like cats and dogs or we ignored each other. Once in a while, one of us would try to start up a friendly conversation. It would only result in a big argument, followed by the silent treatment for days at a time. This is the way it was when my brother decided to move out of the house about six months ago. I thought things would be a lot better when he wasn't around so much, but soon I realized that I really missed him.

One day he came home for dinner, and we were actually getting along! I listened to some records with him, and pretty soon we were talking like crazy. We found out that we did have things in common. Since that night we have become very close. We talk on the phone a lot and do as much together as we can. I think this is a perfect example of trying to make peace.

—Katie F., grade 11

How wonderful it is, how pleasant,
 for God's people to live together in harmony! . . .
That is where the LORD has promised his blessing—
 life that never ends.

—Psalm 133:1,3, TEV

You are the people of God; he loved you and chose you for his own. So then, you must clothe yourselves with compassion, kindness, humility, gentleness, and patience. Be tolerant with one another and forgive one another. . . . And to all these qualities add love, which binds all things together in perfect unity.

—Colossians 3:12-14, TEV

Lord, we want peace to begin at home,
but it's not easy.
When there are conflicts,
help us to share in the responsibility
of solving our problems creatively
and with love.

Help us to recognize in ourselves
whatever irritates others
and destroys peace.

We need you, Lord.

If you are at home in our hearts,
then our homes will be
centers of peace.

26. Taking a Chance on Peace: One Family's Experience

Peace is our work. . . . To everyone, Christians, believers, and men and women of good will, I say: do not be afraid to take a chance on peace, to teach peace. . . . Peace will be the last word of history.

—Pope John Paul II

Writing words of peace for this book did not come about because I am an expert on peace. It came from a need to know just what peacemaking is all about. In fact, as the idea began to germinate, I realized how much there was to learn. At the outset, I had to do battle with negative, un-peaceful forces inside me: You don't know where it will lead. How much will you have to change your life-style? What do you know about peace and justice? Those forces were very real and very scary.

But as the project developed, I began looking for signs of peace in myself and others. In various ways I came to know the peacemakers connected with this book. Many I will never meet personally; others I know very well. One thing we all share is a longing for peace. As each person wrote what peace meant, I had to examine their discoveries in light of my own. And so the process of making a connection between inner peace and outer action began to unfold.

One contact led to another. I was amazed and encouraged by the overwhelming goodness of people pursuing works of peace. They set no limits on what God can accomplish through them, so their efforts know no limits. Many simply saw a need and filled it. Other experiences proved Pope Paul VI's words: "If you want peace, work for justice." The thread running through almost every story was that certain people were deprived of their basic rights and someone decided to do something about it—whether it was providing food, sharing a coat, or giving shelter. Almost always, their works of justice were also works of love—a listening ear, an understanding nod, a warm hug. And they came to realize that all along the way they had been doing acts of peace.

I began sharing my discoveries with my family. That nudging inside to *do* became urgent. In our family prayer we came to realize that the first and obvious thing we could do would be to stop putting off projects we'd been merely considering or picking at for years. And it seemed time to go more consistently beyond the needs of those closest to us. We learned it wasn't scary at all—challenging, yes, but not scary.

We are still discovering projects to do together as a family. Some favorites are visiting old and lonely people and delivering their meals. We also write persons in Congress, and we fast for specific people and intentions. The greatest challenge of all is learning to live more simply, especially at Christmas.

As the peace process unfolds for us, we are discovering new joy and freedom in our small efforts. We believe in Dr. Helen Caldicott's words: "If you give yourselves to the making of peace, you will find great joy." A wonderful new dimension has come into our lives.

Learning about peacemaking is a lifetime journey. It is a slow and sometimes painful process, but we are glad we took a chance and opened our lives to the things that make for peace.

—PCH

The Lord has told us what is good. What he requires of us is this: to do what is just, to show constant love, and to live in humble fellowship with our God.

—Micah 6:8, TEV

Happy are those who work for peace;
God will call them his children! —Matthew 5:9, TEV

Loving Lord, thank you
for the cycles of our lives:
for the times when you carry us through
and for the times
when you challenge us to
take some risks
in order to grow and change.
Often it's easier to keep on doing
what we're used to
than to launch out into the unknown.
But as we learn to open ourselves
to your call to peace,
your challenges become clearer:
Act justly,
love tenderly,
walk with your God.
Then you will be happy,
and you will be mine.
Help us to recognize and depend on
your presence and power, Lord,
so we will not be afraid
to take a chance on peace.

IMAGES OF PEACE

Listening and thinking and speaking about peace aren't enough. We find we must *do* something about it. Often it requires a change in our value system. We can take peaceful actions by beginning to live more simply: by cutting out waste, by fasting so others can have something to eat, and by sharing what has been given to us. In doing these things we will also be conserving the resources of our earth. Perhaps we can take the time to listen to persons who need us, whether they're hungry for food or for companionship. Maybe we can do one peace-filled thing each day, letting "peace fill our heart, our world, our universe" (World Prayer for Peace).

Part Three
Work for Peace

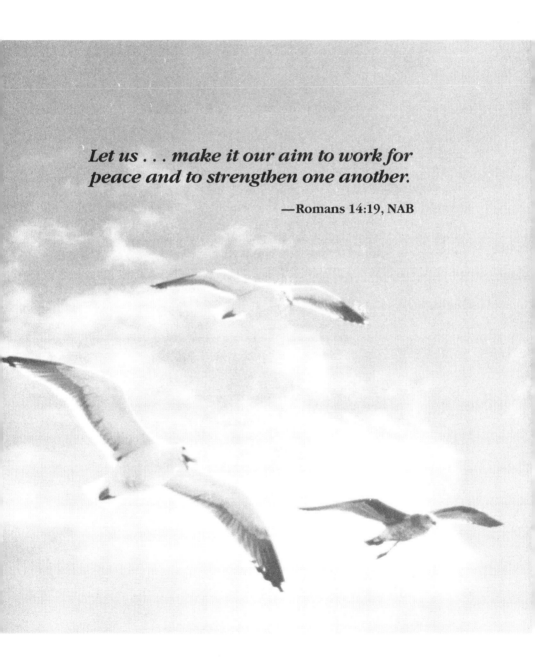

Let us . . . make it our aim to work for peace and to strengthen one another.

—Romans 14:19, NAB

27. Time to Light a Candle

No one has a right to sit down and feel hopeless. There's too much work to do.

—Dorothy Day

Inspired by the Christopher motto, "It is better to light a candle than curse the darkness," John Vincent, twenty-eight, quit his job as a psychiatric technician in California. He moved back to his hometown of Detroit to live and work with severely retarded teenagers. He knew he could not change the whole world, but he was determined to try to change "his" world.

"If you think just about the global reality of famine and nuclear war," he said, "it's very possible to be overwhelmed. But if you concentrate on the shopping-bag lady you see on the street or the arms bazaar in your hometown, or even just on your lonely grandmother or aunt, then it's quite possible to do a little something."

—Adapted from *Christopher World*

When we decide to be a peacemaker,
we see the difference ONE makes:
one apology
    one compliment
      one helper
        one smile
          one song
            one moment
            one Lord
one thing I really don't want to do
    but should.

I'm only ONE person,
    but today
I can do one thing.

—Rod Broding, pastor

Give yourself to the LORD;
    trust in him, and he will help you;
he will make your righteousness
    shine like the noonday sun.

—Psalm 37:5-6, TEV

You are the light of the world.

—Matthew 5:16, RSV

Loving God,
sometimes we're tempted to think
we can't do much by ourselves.
But the way you lived your life
taught us how valuable
one person can be.
Don't let me sit back and complain
or feel hopeless.
Show me today how *I*
can be a person of peace, of hope,
of light and of love,
especially in the dark places.

28. Loosen My Tight Grip

When we die we carry in our clutched hand only what we have given away.

—Peter Maurin

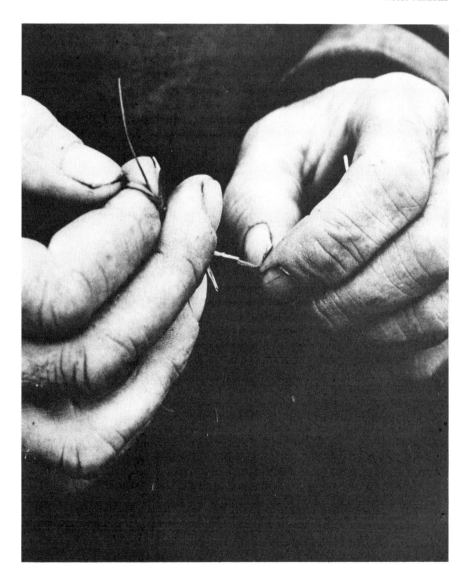

Let not your hand be open to receive
and clenched when it is time to give.

—Sirach 4:31, NAB

The group of believers was one in mind and heart. No one said that
any of his belongings was his own, but they shared with one another
everything they had. With great power the apostles gave witness to
the resurrection of the Lord Jesus, and God poured rich blessings on
them all. There was no one in the group who was in need. Those
who owned fields or houses would sell them, bring the money
received from the sale, and turn it over to the apostles; and the
money was distributed to each one according to his need.

—Acts 4:32-35, TEV

Generous God,
you have gifted me
in so many ways
with the good things of this world.
But sometimes my hands
want to clutch my possessions
tightly,
holding them close
for fear they'll be taken from me.
Lord, loosen my tight grip.
Peel the fingers of greed away
from possessions
that diminish your life in me.

29. *I* Can Make a Difference

The struggle against hunger is one in which everyone can share, for it is a problem of injustice—seeking justice is a constituent part of proclaiming the Gospel. The myths that hunger results from over-population or insufficient production have been exploded. The planet has the productive capacity and technology to feed the population. Hunger is the product of unjust policies and economic structures, of consumerism and materialism, of greed and avarice.

—Moises Sandoval

When I think of world poverty, I usually think that maybe I'm the one who could make a slight difference. Maybe I can feed or make one more person happy. It is hard for people like myself and people who live like I do to give up a lot so we can help the poor.

The very first step we can take is to understand that we are in a position to help others. I can learn more about the causes of hunger and the connection between the United States' policies and hunger, transnational corporations and hunger, and military expenditures and hunger. I can start a project in my school or church to show people how to help the poor. I can volunteer my time at local food shelves or soup kitchens. I can also collect food and money for these food shelves.

I can write to congressmen and let them know my concerns about hunger. If I do this, Congress may understand people's concern about poverty and become more active in this area. I can grow my own fresh vegetables and other foods and donate them to food shelves. I can try to organize a marathon to raise money to help organizations working to feed hungry people. When I get older I could spend my life in a mission in the Third World countries helping the hungry, sick, and dying.

—Mike T., grade 10

If you put an end to oppression, to every gesture of contempt, and to every evil word; if you give food to the hungry and satisfy those who are in need, then the darkness around you will turn to the brightness of noon. And I will always guide you and satisfy you with good things.

—Isaiah 58:9-11, TEV

This is how we know what love is: Christ gave his life for us. We too, then, ought to give our lives for our brothers! If a rich person sees his brother in need, yet closes his heart against his brother, how can he claim that he loves God? My children, our love should not be just words and talk; it must be true love, which shows itself in action.

—1 John 3:16-18, TEV

God, you are generous and just.
It's time I should try to be more like you.

You've opened my eyes and ears
to the cries of others
who are hungry and lonely
and oppressed.

Now open my heart
to the message of your gospel.

Deliver me from *wishing*
good things for the poor.
Make me *do* something
to relieve their cries.

Make it impossible for me
to live with myself
unless I'm doing
some work of peace for you.

30. One to Get Started

It takes one person who cares to get started! Think small and do something to get moving. Growth will come.

—Virgil Nelson, F.O.O.D. Share

When one member of the First Baptist Church in Oak View, California, discovered that only fifty percent of the crops grown in Ventura County were being marketed (the rest was being plowed under), he got together a small group who volunteered to work in the fields and glean whatever produce had been left by employees of wholesale distributors and food processing plants. Bushels of edible fruits and vegetables were collected and stored briefly in a volunteer's garage. Word was spread quickly to senior citizens and to charitable organizations working with persons on limited incomes. The food was then distributed to anyone needing it.

Before long, neighbors were loaning trucks, driving, and doing the gleaning themselves. Senior citizens have become an important element in this group, which took on the name F.O.O.D. Share (Food on

Our Doorsteps). In 1980 the group gleaned and distributed 104 *tons* of produce. In 1981 the total was 346 tons.

This small group has grown to a huge organization and will send ideas to help other groups get started in gleaning, community gardens, obtaining imperfect produce from supermarkets, cooperative bulk purchasing, and food banks (see p. 87).

—PCH

"When you harvest your fields, do not cut the grain at the edges of the fields, and do not go back to cut the heads of grain that were left. Do not go back through your vineyard to gather the grapes that were missed or to pick up the grapes that have fallen; leave them for poor people and foreigners. I am the LORD your God."

—Leviticus 19:9-10, TEV

Each one should give, then, as he has decided, not with regret or out of a sense of duty; for God loves the one who gives gladly. And God is able to give you more than you need, so that you will always have all you need for yourselves and more than enough for every good cause.

—2 Corinthians 9:7-8, TEV

Loving God,
thank you for all your overflowing
love and goodness.
I am amazed at the good you accomplish
through one person or a handful of persons
with a good idea.
It makes me wonder what I can do.
Tune me into you
so good ideas will flow.
Let me never be afraid
to be *one* who is willing to risk
reaching out for that good cause.

31. Peace Is a Life-style

There are two ways to get enough. One is to continue to accumulate more and more. The other is to desire less.

—G. K. Chesterton

Simple life is a mindset. It is a life lived in such a way that one has control over body, mind, and spirit. It is a life lived in such a way as to discern how all living things hang together in a delicately woven chain—the plan of a loving Creator. It is a life that necessitates few material possessions. It enables one to experience the freedom to be oneself. It loves people and uses things. Simple life stresses cooperation instead of competition and strives to exploit no person or group of people. . . . Perhaps someday when I understand what simple life is, I will learn to slow down, to enjoy, to be creative, to give myself freely to others.

—John and Mary Schramm

A group of Quakers have identified four consumption criteria which evoke the essence of voluntary simplicity:
- Does what I own or buy promote activity, self-reliance, and involvement, or does it induce passivity and dependence?
- Are my consumption patterns basically satisfying, or do I buy much that serves no real need?
- How tied is my present job and life-style to installment payments, maintenance and repair costs, and the expectations of others?
- Do I consider the impact of my consumption patterns on other people and on the earth?

—*Alternative Celebrations Catalogue*

The Center for Science in the Public Interest in Washington, D.C., has suggested reasons for living simply. Such a life-style, it says, is:
- Naturalistic—helps us appreciate the serenity of nature, its silence, the changes of season, and its creatures.
- Symbolic—promotes solidarity with the world's poor and reduces the hypocrisy of our current overconsumptive life-style.
- Ecological—reduces our use of resources, lessens pollution, and creates an awareness that we must live in harmony with our world.
- Healthy—lessens tension and anxiety, encourages more rest and relaxation, reduces use of harmful chemicals, creates inner harmony.

- Economical—saves money, reduces the need to work long hours, and increases both number and quality of jobs.
- Spiritual—allows time for meditation and prayer, and rejects materialistic values.
- Social—induces frustration with the limited scope of individual action and incites us to move to social and political action levels.

—Alternative Celebrations Catalogue

"You, LORD, give perfect peace
to those who keep their purpose firm
and put their trust in you."
—Isaiah 26:3, TEV

"So do not start worrying: 'Where will my food come from? or my drink? or my clothes?' (These are the things the pagans are always concerned about.) Your Father in heaven knows that you need all these things. Instead, be concerned above everything else with the Kingdom of God and with what he requires of you, and he will provide you with all these other things."
—Matthew 6:31-33, TEV

Loving God,
by giving us your Son
you have given us the way to peace.
Through Jesus you call us
to break with our present life-styles
of waste and consumerism
and overindulgence.
Help us to take a new look
at our values,
at how we measure success;
help us to use wisely
your gifts of energy
and all the other resources
with which you have blessed us.
Keep us close to your Son
that we might enter the lives
of the poor and the powerless
and help them to help themselves.
God of peace,
give strength to our wills;
give us the determination
to live as Jesus lived
so that others may simply live.

32. Fasting to Be Filled

Fasting, to be truly Christian, must consist in a radical turning of man to God (metanoia) *with a corresponding openness to love and serve his neighbor.*

—George Maloney, S.J.

Deep down inside of me—heart or stomach, I'm not sure—I feel the excessive consumption of food has to stop with me. I have to say *no.* It means not only that I look at my eating habits on Wednesday, but each day I must be more aware of the need to change the consumption patterns I have been taking for granted.... [The authors then quote Bill White, a member of the Order of St. Martin:] Fasting is more than not eating. Not eating is a physical process; fasting involves the total person. A decision not to eat often begins with determination, but a fast requires preparation. For me, this preparation consists of focusing on someone or something. As I think, pray, and anticipate, I begin to identify with other persons, an identification that heightens as the fast progresses.

—John and Mary Schramm

Every Wednesday during Lent, members of one family take turns deciding which part of the meal to omit, such as milk or dessert or even the meatballs from the spaghetti. The amount that these items would cost is put into a decorated "bank." During Holy Week, the money is counted and donated to a needy person, family, or organization that cares for underprivileged persons. The family is considering extending this Lenten custom to the whole year

—PCH

Americans are 6% of the world's population, but we consume nearly 50% of the world's food supply.

—PCH

Did you know that Haiti's grainfed beef supplies our fast-food hamburger chains while Haitians scratch at unproductive soil for their own food?

—PCH

Fast: To abstain from eating all or certain foods,
especially as a religious discipline or as a
means of protest.

—*American Heritage Dictionary*

"The kind of fasting I want is this: Remove the chains of oppression
and the yoke of injustice, and let the oppressed go free. Share your
food with the hungry and open your homes to the homeless poor.
Give clothes to those who have nothing to wear, and do not refuse to
help your own relatives. Then my favor will shine on you like the
morning sun, and your wounds will be quickly healed."

—Isaiah 58:6-8, TEV

The kingdom of God is not a matter of eating or drinking, but of
justice, peace, and the joy that is given by the Holy Spirit. . . . Let us,
then, make it our aim to work for peace and to strengthen one
another.

—Romans 14:17,19, NAB

Lord,
it's so easy to make an idol of food.
If we're following you
and take a good look at your life,
something deep inside us
should remind us that taking in
less food
can actually be more satisfying.
Something deep inside us
should be distressed
that too many fast
because they haven't any food.
You are proof that fasting
clears the mind and strengthens the will.
You are proof that fasting
sets us free to care for others.
Fill us with your Spirit, Lord,
so that our fasting will honor you
and sharpen our senses
as well as our consciences.

33. Example Speaks Loudest

You create peace in the home by being yourself at peace. . . .
it is equally true that you learn to be at peace yourself by
striving to bring peace to the home; you create joy by being
yourself filled with joy. . . . it is what you are that matters
most.

—Gerald Vann, O.P.

A peacemaker is someone who helps people do things. My mom is a peacemaker because she helps people by giving them things they need and inviting them over. She helps with homework and goes to church. She goes to get food for poor people, and she goes to people's houses to help them when they're sick.

—Stacy, grade 3

My grandmother is a peacemaker. Some years ago she was teaching third grade in an inner-city school. Before lunch period one day, there was a big commotion in the back of the room. A little boy was very upset because his lunch was missing from his desk. The next day the very same thing happened, and again every day for about a week. One day when my grandmother went into her desk for her lunch, she found hers gone too. She decided to talk to the class and told them that if someone had been taking the lunches, he or she could come to her after class and no one would know who it was.

The next day, she happened to come into the room while all the children were at recess. She saw one of the little boys taking a lunch from someone else's desk. He started to cry and admitted he had been the one and the reason he had done it was because there wasn't enough food to go around in his family. He was one of ten children, and he just wasn't able to bring his lunch every day. My grandmother took him in her arms and assured him that from now on she would see to it that he had a lunch every day so he wouldn't have to take someone else's. She brought him lunches herself until arrangements could be made through the school. No one knew about this, but it brought peace and happiness to the classroom and most of all to a little boy who didn't have to steal lunches anymore just to be able to eat.

—Jennifer O., grade 10

"Hear, O Israel: The LORD our God is one LORD; and you shall love the LORD your God with all your heart, and with all your soul, and with all your might. And these words which I command you this day shall be upon your heart; and you shall teach them diligently to your children, and shall talk of them when you sit in your house, and when you walk by the way, and when you lie down, and when you rise."

—Deuteronomy 6:4-7, RSV

The wisdom from above is pure first of all; it is also peaceful, gentle, and friendly; it is full of compassion and produces a harvest of good deeds; it is free from prejudice and hypocrisy. And goodness is the harvest that is produced from the seeds the peacemakers plant in peace.

—James 3:17-18, TEV

Lord, it takes a lot of living
to understand we are constantly
passing something on to others
by who we are.
It's an awesome challenge;
but if we try to be
authentic and real,
the best we can be,
example will take care of itself.

Help us realize that much of what we do
is taken with small steps—little things
that make a big difference:
"I'm sorry"; "I care"; "I love you."
Help us risk taking time
to be persons of joy, of peace,
and of love.

Then what we have to pass on
will be you.

34. Don't Wait for George to Do It

I wondered why somebody didn't do something for peace. . . .
Then I realized that I am somebody.

—Anonymous

Harry carefully works his way over the icy sidewalk toward the basement of the old church. He has spent the day searching for a welding job (or any job) but hasn't found one. He has just finished his one meal of the day, served hot and free in the parish school cafeteria.

"One more night," he tells himself. "Just one more night I'll sleep here. For sure, I'll find a job tomorrow so I can get a place of my own."

Harry has been saying that to himself every night for two months. But still no job. He is grateful for a warm place to go, at least at night, even if it is a church library. He has a place to go because the pastor, Father Ed, decided some time ago that as long as he has space to spare, at least some of the homeless can have a warm, dry place to come to at night.

—PCH

Teresa brought her eighteen-month-old baby down from her room to the nursery on the first floor of the old convent. A smiling volunteer took the baby and held her for a moment, then placed her near some other young children. "She'll be fine, Teresa. Enjoy your class."

Teresa smiled and pulled her sweater close around her as she walked down the hall to the large informal room at the end. It was nearly filled with young mothers like herself. Each of them had recently broken away from an abusive or co-dependent relationship and were living in this renovated building to learn how to become more self-sufficient.

Teresa had made a commitment to try this with her new baby for three months. She was learning some skills and dreamed of getting enough background and experience here in this supportive environment to make it on her own by summer. One door had closed to her, but another had opened because a small group of nuns and laypeople were determined not to let an empty but usable building go to waste.

—PCH

Canned goods were quickly disappearing at the emergency food shelves in a large city. The staff dreaded thinking that they would soon have to tell needy people they were out of food.

Then Joan got an idea. She knew a professional football playoff game was scheduled in town for the following Monday evening. She got staff and volunteers together, obtained permission to request canned goods for donation at a public function, and set up depots at each entrance to the stadium. Through the media, everyone attending the upcoming game was invited to bring one canned item to go on food shelves. The response was overwhelming. Thousands of cans were donated. This sparked a huge campaign by corporations based in that city to make sure the food shelves would never be empty again. The goal of that campaign was 250 million pounds of food. They actually collected more than 600 million pounds.

—PCH

Fill us at daybreak with your kindness. . . .
And may the gracious care of the Lord our God be ours;
    prosper the work of our hands for us!

—Psalm 90:14,17, NAB

My brothers, what good is it to profess faith without practicing it?
Such faith has no power to save one, has it? If a brother or sister has
nothing to wear and no food for the day, and you say to them,
"Good-bye and good luck! Keep warm and well fed," but do not meet
their bodily needs, what good is that? So it is with the faith that does
nothing in practice. It is thoroughly lifeless.

—James 2:14-17, NAB

Lord,
most of the time it's easier
to walk around talking
about the sorry state of those in need
than it is to do something about it.

It's much easier to talk about it
than to slow down and
look inside ourselves and ask,
"What can *I* do?"

Help me not to leave
the works of peace up to others
but to put my actions where my faith is.

Tune me in
to what *you* want *me* to do.
Today. Now.

35. See What God Can Do Through You

God has no one but us to do the very things we ask him for.

—Louis Evely

Rarely do parish workers who serve the needy see money multiply before their eyes as Sister Mildred did. She often had to ask charitable organizations for donations, and last November the Knights of Columbus responded generously with a check for $600. Their only stipulation was that it be used for food and clothes for the poor.

Around that same time, another friend in a neighboring inner-city parish was preparing her annual Thanksgiving dinner for anyone needing a good meal. This woman somehow managed to feed 1,000 people every year. She would collect donations of food from as many places as possible and supply from her own pocket whatever else was needed.

Sister Mildred thought this might be the place for the whole $600, but felt she should check first with the organization. The members of the board listened carefully and responded, "Sister, you keep the money for as many individuals as you feel need it. We're going to give a separate check of $600 to help that wonderful lady pay for all that food!"

—PCH

The widow went and did as Elijah had told her, and all of them had enough food for many days. As the Lord had promised through Elijah, the bowl did not run out of flour nor did the jar run out of oil.

—1 Kings 17:15, TEV

Then Jesus took the five loaves and the two fish, looked up to heaven, and gave thanks to God. He broke the loaves and gave them to his disciples to distribute to the people. He also divided the two fish among them all. Everyone ate and had enough.

—Mark 6:41-42, TEV

Loving Lord,
you are so generous
that once we ask you for help,
we never know
how wonderful your help might be.

Multiply your gifts in us.
Intensify our response to your gifts.
Help us to trust you so much
that we never doubt
that *you* are the one with the power.

Teach us to allow you
to work in us
so we can experience
how exciting it is
when you take over.

36. Peace Is a Presence: Yours

First there must be order and harmony within your own mind. Then this order will spread to your family, then to the community, and finally to your entire kingdom. Only then can you have peace and harmony.

—Confucius

Mary's doctor ordered her to stay in bed for most of each day for the remainder of her pregnancy. She couldn't imagine how she'd be able to stand it for four months. Mary had always wanted to manage things for herself.

There were serious reasons behind her need for rest. One was a weak heart. She also had uterine tumors. She gave in to the doctor's orders, thinking she'd manage to take care of the family and still rest. She tried cooking the meals and keeping the house in order—for a while—until she had another heart seizure and became so weak she had to stay in bed all day, every day.

Members of her parish and other friends wanted to help. She still insisted that her husband and boys could manage without outside help. Finally, a member of her Scripture prayer group confronted her. "Mary, you need to let us help you. We need to help you as much as you need us." In tears and pain, Mary gave in. Dozens of people began preparing meals, cleaning house, sending cards and tapes, flowers, and books, and constantly looking in on her, praying for her and with her.

Mary and her family were in awe. Everyone was awed by the great number of people who were so willing and happy to be involved.

As Mary grew weaker and more dependent, she also grew in wisdom and peace. "I realize now how selfish I was not to let other people help me. When I get to feeling better, I'll need to do things for others too. I'll surely feel rejected or hurt if they don't let me help."

Weeks turned into months. Mary's baby had become everyone's baby. "It will be the best attended baptism in the history of the parish," they said proudly.

One day a friend asked, "Does all that coming and going ever wear you out?" Mary responded, "Oh, no, not at all. Each person has become special. I'm amazed at how important our presence is to one another. I'm encouraged when each person is present here with me, and I know they're here because they want to be. They all give me strength by being here. I see God's love and care coming to us through each person."

But everyone who came to this house received something in return. Mary's patience and acceptance of her illness, her newly learned ability to receive help, and her family's loving care of her inspired each visitor to a new understanding of how God makes his love and presence known through each of his people.

On Thanksgiving night, Mary delivered a tiny, perfectly formed, beautiful baby. To everyone's delight she at last had a girl.

A few months later, the tumors were successfully removed, and Mary's health steadily improved. The family was drawn even closer together by the presence of the baby girl, and the love of friends and community continued to pour in. The little child became a symbol of the love and care of the community and a crowning, loving reminder of God's presence among us.

—PCH

The LORD who created you says,
"Do not be afraid—I will save you.
I have called you by name—you are mine.
When you pass through deep waters, I will be with you;
     your troubles will not overwhelm you."

—Isaiah 43:1,2, TEV

In all our trouble and suffering we have been encouraged about you. . . . It was your faith that encouraged us, because now we really live if you stand firm in your life in union with the Lord. Now we can give thanks to our God for you. We thank him for the joy we have in his presence because of you.

—1 Thessalonians 3:7-9, TEV

Lord,
we can learn so much life and love
from one another.
But sometimes we are tempted
to take it all on by ourselves.
We forget how much we need you.
We forget how much we need one another.
Open up our awareness of you
and of those around us.
Let us feel the peace and love
of your presence
as we become more present
to one another.

37. Be an Earth Caretaker

Teach your children what we have taught our children, that the earth is our mother. Whatever befalls the earth, befalls the children of the earth. . . . The earth does not belong to us; we belong to the earth. . . . So love it as we have loved it. Care for it as we have cared for it. And with all your strength, with all your mind, with all your heart, preserve it for your children, and love it . . . as God loves us all.

—Chief Seattle of the Suquamish Nation, 1854

Recognizing that the earth and the fullness thereof is a gift from God, and that we are called to cherish, nurture and provide loving steward-ship for the earth's resources,

And recognizing that life itself is a gift, and a call to responsibility, joy and celebration, I make the following declarations:
1. I declare myself to be a world citizen.
2. I commit myself to lead an ecologically sound life.
3. I commit myself to occupational responsibility. I will seek to avoid the creation of products which work others harm.
4. I commit myself to personal renewal through meditation, prayer and reflection.
5. I affirm the gift that is my body, and pledge that I will attend to its proper nourishment and physical fitness.
6. I pledge myself to examine continually my relations with others and to attempt to relate honestly, morally and lovingly with those around me.
7. I commit myself to responsible participation in a community of faith.
8. I commit myself to leading a life of creative simplicity, and to share my personal wealth with the world's poor.
9. I commit myself to join with others in the reshaping of institutions in order to bring about a more just global society in which each person has full access to the needed resources for their physical, emotional, intellectual and spiritual growth.

—The Shakertown Pledge

Your land . . . belongs to God, and you are like foreigners who are allowed to make use of it.

—Leviticus 25:23, TEV

From the very beginning the Word was with God. Through him God made all things; not one thing in all creation was made without him. The Word was the source of life, and this life brought light to mankind.

—John 1:3-4, TEV

God, our Creator,
your life is the source of our life
and of all creation.
How have we wandered so far
from the covenant you made with us?

Why do we turn away from you
when you are all good?
Why do we do violence to one another
when we are each your work of love?
How do we dare to desecrate the earth
you have so wonderfully made?

Lord, set us on fire with your
creating and redeeming Spirit.

Let our faith be so strong
that we will be a sign of hope,
of harmony, and of wholeness
in this mixed-up world.

Let our love for one another
and for all you have made
show how much we love you
and praise you
and thank you.

38. A Celebration of Love: Words of Mother Teresa

God has not called me to be successful. He has called me to be faithful.

The beginning of love is always small things done with great love.

Take the trouble to talk to the poor. Then you will have the courage to give.

Some people came to Calcutta and before leaving, they begged me: "Tell us something that will help us to live our lives better." And I said: "Smile at each other. Smile at your wife and at your husband, at your children and at each other. It doesn't matter who it is. That will help you to grow up in greater love for each other."

Our works are nothing but works of peace.

In a rare interview on TV, Mother Teresa was asked what message she has for the women of America. She replied: "Woman was created to love. She is a special gift of God because her heart is full of love. God has given her power to create life. It takes only one woman to make a difference. She was created to love and be loved. That love must be put into action. She must love her family with an undivided love. A mother can make the family or break the family."

Money, I never think of it. It always comes. The Lord sends it. We do His work; He provides the means. If He does not give us the means, that shows He does not want the work. So why worry?

—Mother Teresa

Thoughtfulness is the beginning of great sanctity. If you learn this art of being thoughtful, you will become more and more Christ-like, for His heart was meek and He always thought of others.

Never let anything so fill you with sorrow as to make you forget the joy of Christ risen.

The biggest disease today is not leprosy or tuberculosis, but rather the feeling of being unwanted, uncared for and deserted by everybody.

—Malcolm Muggeridge

The spirit of the Lord GOD is upon me,
      because the LORD has anointed me;
He has sent me to bring glad tidings to the lowly,
      to heal the brokenhearted,
To proclaim liberty to the captives,
      and release to the prisoners.   —Isaiah 61:1, NAB

"When you give a lunch or dinner, do not invite your friends or brothers or your relatives or your rich neighbors—for they will invite you back, and in this way you will be paid for what you did. When you give a feast, invite the poor, the crippled, the lame, and the blind; and you will be blessed, because they are not able to pay you back."

—Luke 14:12-14, TEV

Loving God, thank you
for the love and faithfulness
of Mother Teresa.
There is so much need everywhere—
I often feel overwhelmed.
Part of me wants to shut misery out,
turn it off, or at least
turn it away from me.
But the gospel part of me
wonders and prods and impels:
You can't call yourself Christian
if you're glued to the seat
of your meditation chair.
You can't look at the lives
of desperate people,
and go on as if this were acceptable.
Then I look at all Mother Teresa is doing,
and I wonder where to begin.
I hear you say through her:
Begin with love for the person next to you.
One step at a time.

39. Try Something Different This Christmas

One of the exciting aspects of an alternative Christmas is that it frees you from the things you always "had to do," and lets you start things in new and different ways. You can pick and choose the things you like best over a few years, and you will have your own traditions, which can be for your family, your neighborhood or your church.

—*Alternative Celebrations Catalogue*

It was Christmas Eve. As we stepped off the elevator in the high-rise, the halls seemed barren and narrow. "Low-income housing has only the essentials, it seems," I commented as my family and I searched for 707. We knocked and waited, excited and a little nervous to be bringing the first of our needy recipients a carefully prepared hot turkey dinner, a poinsettia, and a TV tray wrapped in a bow. Someone inside shuffled to the door and opened it. A tall, elderly man smiled shyly as we said, "Merry Christmas, Mr. Belgarde! We're from the Little Brothers, and we have some gifts for you."

He beckoned us into the single room apartment, saying, "Someone called to say you'd be coming. It sure is nice." My husband asked him how he was getting along.

"Oh, fine. I have to."

My son placed the TV tray in front of a chair and said, "Maybe you can eat your dinner while you watch . . . uh . . . well, while you listen to the radio," he said lamely, noticing there was no television.

"Sure, I just might sit down to eat this nice meal. It's hot! Usually I just open a can and eat it cold."

I noticed a deck of cards on the table. "Do you like to play solitaire?" He nodded.

"We like it too. Maybe we can come back and play double solitaire with you some day."

"Yup. Sure. I'd like that."

It was getting a little awkward standing, so we made motions to leave, wishing him a happy holiday again. He replied, "It was sure nice of you to bring this. Thanks. Thanks a lot."

I didn't realize until later the irony of my question: "Do you like to play solitaire?"

—PCH

Olive was the one who cheered *us* up—even though *we* were visiting *her.* She waved to us from her sofa as we came in.

"Hello, hello. Nice to see you. Would you like some candy?"

She oohed and aahed over the meal and gifts and had us arrange all of them on her table. She proudly pointed out a wall displaying drawings made by her grandchildren, and she chattered continually. Mostly she complained about her age.

"I'm ninety-seven years old," she said shrilly. "Why am I still here? I can't see. I can't hear. I can't walk right. What am I good for?" Then she laughed in a cackling sort of way.

My daughter, thinking she might console her, said, "My grandma is eighty-seven, Olive. I wish she could meet you."

"Why, she's just a kid!" Olive cried out, and cackled again.

As we stood to leave I took her hand and said, "Olive, I think you're still here so you could make *us* happy. We're so glad to meet you. You're really special."

Olive softened visibly. "Oh, thank you, dear. I didn't mean all that. But I do wonder why I'm still around."

—PCH

Kindness shown to the poor is an act of worship. —Proverbs 14:31, TEV

"'When, Lord, did we ever see you hungry and feed you, or thirsty and give you a drink? When did we ever see you a stranger and welcome you in our homes, or naked and clothe you? When did we ever see you sick or in prison, and visit you?' The King will reply, 'I tell you, whenever you did this for one of the least important of these brothers of mine, you did it for me!'"

—Matthew 25:37-40, TEV

Lord Jesus,
sometimes we get so used
to one way of doing things
it's hard to change.
Enlighten what is dark in us.
Help us to understand
that you are calling,
inviting us to a new dimension
in our living.

Set us free
so that we can
hear your voice
or see your face
in those who are in need,
especially your lonely poor.
Then, like you, we will
be peace for them.

40. Shalom:
Wholeness, Harmony, Health, Peace

In his will is our peace. — Dante

As a college student in 1967, I had the privilege of spending a summer working at a resort in Switzerland. It was a dream come true. It was fascinating to meet so many people of different nationalities. The ones I was most taken with were the Jews who had emigrated to Israel and who vacationed in Switzerland because they could not bear to return to their native Germany—the site of memories of the '30s and '40s. One day I talked with a man who was interested in the fact that American students were working in Europe. I was impressed with his kind and gentle manner.

One morning I noticed that this family was leaving. I set the trays aside and walked over to tell them how much I had enjoyed visiting with them. The man said he had also enjoyed meeting me. That was his job with an international organization out of Amsterdam—meeting and talking with young people from all over the world.

I asked, "Is this to help students find jobs or gain entrance into universities abroad?"

"No," he said. "It's simply to bring people together for talks and discussions on promoting peace and better understanding in the world."

"Oh, I think that's just great," I replied. "One thing I've learned from my summer working and traveling here is that until you've lived and worked with persons from different countries and backgrounds, you can never really understand their feelings and problems. I think the only way we can have peace in this world is to have persons of different nationalities living and working together."

He clasped my hand in both of his, smiled, and nodded. I told him we would be in Amsterdam later that summer. "Could we visit you at the organization where you work?"

He said I should just ask for him when we arrived.

"And who should I ask for?"

"Just ask for Frank," he said.

With typical American casualness I said, "Frank . . . ?"

He replied softly, "I'm Anne Frank's father."

Tears spilled from my eyes. I had read all about Anne Frank's experiences and death in the Nazi concentration camp, and I was overwhelmed when I realized the words I had just spoken and the relevance they had to his own life. All I could mumble was how honored I was to meet him.

He shook my hand again and said, "I'm happy to hear what you've said. If people could remember the ideals they had when they were seventeen and live by them till they were seventy, the world would be a better place. So stick to your ideals."

Mr. Frank and his wife returned to Basel, Switzerland, and I took the trays back to the kitchen, shaking and profoundly moved by this man who had tried so bravely to hide his family from the Nazis and who after two years was discovered and saw them cut down. This man could not only forgive and love again, but was directing all his energies to preventing such atrocities from ever happening again.

Over the years that conversation from a chance encounter has reminded me again and again to put my hurt aside—to forgive, to love, to seek to understand, and to move forward.

—Diane Spieker, parent

Once more God will send us his spirit. The wasteland will become fertile, and fields will produce rich crops. Everywhere in the land righteousness and justice will be done. Because everyone will do what is right, there will be peace and security forever. God's people will be free from worries, and their homes peaceful and safe.

—Isaiah 32:15-18, TEV

He is our peace.

—Ephesians 2:14, RSV

Lord, our faithful God,
we can't delay the work of peace
any longer.
Never have we needed it so much
and found it so difficult to attain.
Sometimes it seems the dark powers
of hate and irrational thinking
will forever prevent
a real and lasting peace.
But we know your love is greater
than all the powers of darkness.
Enlighten whatever is dark
within each of us.
Release us from our violence and fears
and fill us with your wholeness
and health and harmony,
your peace.
We believe in your promise.
We will walk in your light and love.
Amen. Come, Lord Jesus!
You are our peace.

Published Sources Used

I gratefully acknowledge the published sources used in this book. When only the author's name is given, it means either that the source is so well known as to make further identification needless or that I have been unable to track down the source. In the latter case, any additional information discovered later will be noted in a future printing.

Part One
1. Irenaeus.
2. Robert Faricy, S.J. *Praying* (Minneapolis: Winston, 1979).
3. Leo Cardinal Suenens.
4. Thomas Merton, as quoted in James H. Forest, "Merton's Peacemaking," *Sojourners,* Dec. 1978.
5. Dorothy Corkille Briggs. *Your Child's Self-Esteem* (New York: Dolphin Books, Doubleday, 1975).
   Letter taken from *Pennsylvania Law Enforcement Journal.*
6. Martin Luther King, Jr. *Strength to Love* (Philadelphia: Fortress, 1963).
7. Ronald J. Sider. *Rich Christians in an Age of Hunger* (Downers Grove, Ill.: Intervarsity Press, 1977).
8. Joseph Allegretti. "On Loving the Russians," *Sojourners,* Nov. 1982.
9. Dom Helder Câmara. *The Desert Is Fertile* (Maryknoll, N.Y.: Orbis, 1974).
   American Heritage Dictionary, New College Edition (New York: Houghton Mifflin, 1976).
10. Edward Farrell. *Prayer Is a Hunger* (Denville, N.J.: Dimension Books, 1972).
11. John Howard Yoder. *The Politics of Jesus* (Grand Rapids: Eerdmans, 1972).
    Joseph J. Fahey. *Peace, War, and the Christian Conscience* (New York: The Christophers, 1982).
12. Chuck Walters. "Prayer Alone Will Sustain Peacemakers over the Long Run," *Catholic Bulletin,* Jan. 13, 1981.
13. Ladislaus Boros. *In Time of Temptation* (New York: Herder, 1968).

Part Two
14. Reinhold Niebuhr.
15. Teilhard de Chardin.
16. (No sources.)
17. Henri Nouwen and Walter J. Gaffney. *Aging* (New York: Image Books, 1974).
    "Dear Abby" column.

18. Edward Everett Hale.
19. Dietrich Bonhoeffer. *Life Together* (New York: Harper and Row, 1954).
20. Kahlil Gibran. *The Prophet* (New York: Alfred A. Knopf, 1972).
21. Joseph Roy, as quoted in a church bulletin.
22. Leon Bloy.
    Christopher News Notes, Jan.-Feb. 1982, No. 259 (New York: The Christophers).
    Norman Cousins. *Anatomy of an Illness* (New York: W. W. Norton, 1979).
23. Henry Wadsworth Longfellow.
    Media Tip Sheet (Washington, D.C.: Office of Human Development Services, n.d.).
24. Richard Barnet.
    Jim Wallis. "Peace Pentecost," *Sojourners*, March 1982.
    Peace Packet (New York: The Christophers, 1982).
25. Dolores Curran. *Traits of a Healthy Family* (Minneapolis: Winston, 1983).
26. Pope John Paul II.

Part Three

27. Dorothy Day.
    Christopher World (New York: The Christophers).
28. Peter Maurin.
29. Moises Sandoval. "Hunger, a Problem of Injustice," *Maryknoll*, Nov. 1982.
30. Virgil Nelson. F.O.O.D. Share (P.O. Box 4596, Ventura, Calif. 93004).
31. G. K. Chesterton.
    John and Mary Schramm. *Things That Make for Peace* (Minneapolis: Augsburg, 1976).
    Alternative Celebrations Catalogue, 4th edition (Bloomington, Ind.: Alternatives, 1978), quoting *99 Ways to a Simple Lifestyle*.
32. George Maloney, S.J. *A Return to Fasting* (Pecos, N.M.: Dove, 1974).
    John and Mary Schramm (as in #31).
33. Gerald Vann, O.P. *The Divine Pity* (New York: Image Books, 1961).
34. (No sources.)
35. Louis Evely. *Teach Us How to Pray* (New York: Paulist, 1967).
36. Confucius.
37. Chief Seattle, as quoted by Kathleen and James McGinnis. *Parenting for Peace and Justice* (New York: Orbis, 1981).
    The Shakertown Pledge, drawn up by staff members of a religious retreat center in Shakertown, Kentucky, in 1973; quoted in

Alternative Celebrations Catalogue (see #31).

38. Mother Teresa, as quoted in newspapers and magazines, and by Malcolm Muggeridge, *Something Beautiful for God* (New York: Harper and Row, 1971).

39. *Alternative Celebrations Catalogue* (see #31).

40. Dante.